Man of Two Worlds

A German Family
Confronts the American Dream

Ray Grasshoff

Contents

Appendices

PREFACE

Texas, just as the rest of the United States, owes much of its development to a large cadre of immigrants from foreign lands. Even today, immigrants continue to bring their desire for a better life, their work ethic, and their culture to the Lone Star State, as they have for hundreds of years. Despite geographic, legal, and financial hurdles through many decades, new generations of immigrants continue to cut out a new life in a new land, contributing to an ever-evolving melting pot of human knowledge and experience that make the state a success.

Through those decades, many different groups of people have made their mark, with their influence rising and falling over the years, usually as each group accounts for substantially more or less of the state's population over time. In the mid to late 1800s, perhaps no other single group had more emerging influence in Texas than people from the European duchies, principalities, and kingdoms known collectively today as Germany.

German immigrants to Texas accounted for approximately 5 percent of the state's population throughout the second half of the 19th century, and that influence continues to weight the state's population more recently, too.[1] More than 17 percent of the state's population claimed some German ancestry in 1990, according to that year's census.[2]

Fortunately, those 19th century German immigrants left a relatively rich trove of written works documenting their experiences and influences in Texas. There were German- and English-language newspapers, minutes of organizations such as the Cat Spring Agricultural Society in Austin County, census data, memoirs, letters to and from family members, and similar documents that tell us much about their activities.

---

[1] Jordan, Terry G. "Germans." *The Handbook of Texas Online*. January 21, 2009. <http://www.tshaonline.org/handbook/online/articles/GG/png2.html>

[2] Ibid.

In particular, memoirs and collections of letters written among the Germans enlighten us about their daily lives. Those documents detail many aspects of their activities – such as what they ate, how they endured Texas weather, where they traveled, and more.

Far less common are personal letters that touch on emotions, especially the emotional toll taken by the disruption of lives in the Old World when a younger generation left for the New World and showed no desire to return. The mental adjustment was monumental, with parents losing their children and grandchildren to a distant land, usually without any hope of seeing them again. Emigration of sons and daughters also meant that they would be unavailable to carry on family businesses and farms or help the parents cope with illness and old age, all perhaps traditional roles for the younger generation in largely place-bound European families of the earlier part of the 19th century.

The Kempe family of Sayda, in the Kingdom of Saxony, was one of many families that faced these trials. Eldest child Wilhelm Friedrich Kempe and his sister Auguste, both in their 20s, left their homeland in 1854 for the promise of a new and better life across the Atlantic. In Sayda, they left their widowed father August, 54; their younger sister, Bertha, then 10; and their younger brother, Alwin, then 8.

Both Wilhelm and Auguste married within a few years of their arrival in Texas, and Wilhelm also applied for U.S. citizenship. Clearly, there was no turning back for them. Not only had they left their homeland physically, but spiritually and emotionally as well.

The new life and new opportunities that attracted so many Germans to the U.S. in the mid-1800s was upset for many of them by the Civil War in the 1860s. And so it was for Wilhelm and Auguste and their new families as they coped with those years of chaos.

Following the war, many letters crossed the Atlantic to Wilhelm as he renewed his commitment to his new life on a new frontier. In particular, the letters written by his father and sister reflect considerable emotional pain and turmoil at his absence. With nearly every letter to Wilhelm, they levy a "guilt trip," even if inadvertently, that few could resist. More than anything, it seems, the father wants Wilhelm to return to Sayda and take over the family farm.

Eventually, and decades after first making his home in Texas, Wilhelm crossed the Atlantic to Germany for a visit to his native Sayda. Before returning back to America, he writes to his wife – who has remained behind in Texas – with some surprising observations about life in Germany compared to life in Texas.

Friends, acquaintances, and cousins also write letters to Wilhelm in Texas through the years, but often for reasons other than exchanging family news. Although their letters suggest that they lead largely successful lives in Saxony, they want to join Wilhelm in Texas, and they seek his advice.

The Kempe letters provide a remarkable insight into strong emotional tugs faced by people making these decisions, as well as the people around them. Not only did emigration affect the emigrants. It also affected family members left behind in Europe. They grieved for decades over the loss of their children and siblings. Those disruptions come alive through the writings of the real people who faced these severe disruptions in their lives.

My initial interest in Wilhelm Friedrich Kempe and his family stems from the fact that he is my great-great-grandfather. I grew up in Fayette County, Texas, where he lived much of his life.

Ray Grasshoff
Austin, Texas

TRANSLATING THE LETTERS

Translations of these letters are difficult because they are written in an old German script that is no longer in use. This script is notoriously tricky to decipher into modern German, which a translator must do before translating the German into English. The difficulty arises because many letters of the script alphabet look very similar. Even slight variations in handwriting style or skill can produce different interpretations by different translators. Also, any particular writer might pen a particular letter of the alphabet one way in one letter, then another way in another letter.

These difficulties in translation pose a special problem for identifying names that are unknown to translators and others today. The best example is the surname of Wilhelm Kempe's cousins. In the original early-1960s English translations,[3] which all appear to be the work of the same person hired by Wilhelm's descendants at that time, the cousins' surname was interpreted as "Niezel" in most letters, but as "Naegel" in one and as "Mogel" in another. It appears that the translator didn't recognize the identical surname of a brother and sisters who wrote in their different handwriting styles in their separate letters. More recently, another translator, studying one of the few letters for which legible copies exist today, became certain that the correct surname is "Weigel." That is the name used here. Efforts to confirm the name by examining records available from Germany have been unsuccessful.

Other errors seem to have entered as the English translations were transcribed and/or typed. For example, the March 17, 1876 letter to Wilhelm's son from his uncle John Mayer contains this sentence in the original translation: *"The two girls and one boy are the only two engineer mans in school"* This rather cryptic sentence almost certainly should be *"The two girls and one boy are the only two Germans in school,"* and that change has been made in this book. The genesis of

---

[3] Kempe, Gladys T., ed. *Letters to and from William Frederick Kempe*. Incorporates translations, ca. 1961 (Unpublished; document exists only as photocopy in possession of unknown number of Kempe family members and possibly others.)

such an error is easy to understand if a stenograph machine, commonly used by court reporters, was used to produce the transcribed letters. Keys on a stenograph machine keyboard represent sounds rather than letters, as on a typewriter keyboard, and the strokes that would represent "engineer mans" and "Germans" are identical for most court reporters.

Another example of a translation or typing error is the original reference to "Russia" rather than "Prussia" in a part of the July 20, 1870 letter to Wilhelm and others from his brother Alwin.

Regrettably, the original letters, plus what might have been at least part of an early diary (see "Preface") kept by Wilhelm before he left Europe, have been lost or destroyed since the first translations were made nearly half a century ago. Efforts in recent years to locate the original letters, digitize them, and make permanent electronic records of them have been unsuccessful. Some family members fear that they have been destroyed by others.

As a result, the most "original" documents available to researchers today appear to be photocopies made with the 1960s translations. Those photocopies have faded so much that they are largely unreadable, however. New translations, which could provide new information, are impossible for most – but not all – of them.

A few of the more legible photocopies have been re-translated since 2000, providing some new insights (such as establishing "Weigel" as a more likely surname for Wilhelm's cousins). Those new translations are incorporated when the translators are certain about their new interpretations, or where those new interpretations clearly appear to be more accurate.

PEOPLE IN THE LETTERS

The letters are from various friends and relatives, and mention still other people. Their relationships to Wilhelm F. Kempe:

In Germany

August Dietel – brother-in-law; husband of Bertha Kempe Dietel.

Bertha Kempe Dietel – sister; wife of August Dietel.

Karl Dietel – nephew; daughter of August and Bertha Kempe Dietel.

Marie Dietel – niece; daughter of August and Bertha Kempe Dietel.

Clementine Weigel Einert [nickname **"Zienel**?] – cousin; wife of Friedrich Einert.

Friedrich Einert – husband of cousin Clementine Weigel Einert.

Maria Einert – niece living with Friedrich and Clementine Weigel Einert; the biological daughter of one of Clementine's sisters.

August Ferdinand Einhorn – acquaintance of the Kempe family.

Alwin Kempe – brother.

August Friedrich Kempe – father.

Christel Weigel Peterlein – cousin; wife of a man surnamed Peterlein.

Amalie Kempe Weigel – aunt.

Mienel Weigel – cousin

Edward Weigel – cousin.

Hermann Weigel – cousin.

Maria Weigel – cousin

In Texas

Frederike Laas Kempe – wife.

Auguste "Gustel" Kempe Mayer – sister.

John [Johann] Mayer – brother-in-law; husband of Auguste Kempe Mayer.

Marie Mayer – niece; daughter of Johann "John" and Auguste Kempe Mayer.

Anna Mayer – niece; daughter of Johann "John" and Auguste Kempe Mayer.

Part I

The Man
and His Life

Chapter One

WILHELM FRIEDRICH KEMPE

Wilhelm Friedrich[4] Kempe was born October 16, 1828, at Sayda, in the Kingdom of Saxony (part of today's Germany) to August Friedrich Kempe and Christiane Hoepfner Kempe. August was a landowner and a farmer. The Kempe family had lived in the area for many generations.

Sayda, with a population today of approximately 2,200 people, is in the Erzgebirge (Ore Mountains) region of southeastern Germany, very near the present-day border between Germany and the Czech Republic. It is surrounded by low, forested mountains, with open pastureland nearby as well.

As a young adult, Wilhelm worked in different parts of Germany to earn money to emigrate to America. Apparently he kept a journal during that part of his life, but only several passages, translated into English more than a century later, in the early 1960s, survive:

"[Sarburg?], *here I was signed into my country, but far yet from getting there"* [Translators note: "This page consisted of numerous names of cities that he traveled through and worked in to get money to continue on."]

"Querfurt, here I have been working from May 16, 1852, until April 13, 1853. I went on my journey again to Altstadt, Sangerhausen, Artern, Frankenhausen. Here I worked again from April 16 until June 7, 1853."

"Now back in [Ardern?], Dresden, capital and residence of my native country. Here I worked again from June 18, 1853 until February 14, 1854. Here in my last function in Germany, I have many friends and experienced a lot of

---

[4] In many papers and documents compiled by his descendants in the 1960s, Wilhelm's middle name is provided alternatively as the English language version "Frederick." Only the middle initial "F." appears in almost all early records, however. It is clearly "Friedrich" in the baptismal records for his first two children, so that name is used here.

fun. Now I have decided to emigrate to America, with my sister Auguste and the family Preissler, and this resolution made me quit my job. So with God Almighty I will start my travel to America February 23."

Wilhelm was 26 when he came to Texas in 1854 with his younger sister, Auguste, who was 20. A short family history that appears in a history of Shiner,[5] Lavaca County, Texas (where many of Wilhelm's descendants lived) indicates that he arrived as early as 1843, and the 1910 census indicates 1842. Both dates are inaccurate. The correct date of 1854 appears in the short item from his journal, in his application for citizenship, and in the 1900 U.S. census. However, neither his name nor that of his sister has been identified on passenger lists of ships arriving at any American port. But many such lists for arrivals at Galveston, Texas – a possible point of entry for them – were destroyed in a hurricane that struck that city in 1900. Possibly they came ashore at Indianola, a seaport below Galveston on the Texas coast. No passenger lists exist for this port, however, since it was a secondary entry point –

Wilhelm Friedrich Kempe
1828-1920

carrying immigrants who had technically arrived first at Galveston, New Orleans, or elsewhere before boarding a smaller ship for Indianola's shallower waters.

Wilhelm and Auguste settled in Austin County near its present-day border with Colorado and Fayette counties, in an area where many

---

[5] Kempe, Mrs. P.O. "Kempe, William Frederick, Sr." *Shiner, Texas: The First 100 Years, 1887-1987.* (Curtis Media Corp., Dallas, for Shiner History Book Committee, 1986). F148. 217-218.

other German immigrants lived. He applied for citizenship on April 27, 1858, and was naturalized as a U.S. citizen in 1860.

On December 6, 1856, Auguste, then 22, married fellow German immigrant John [Johann] Mayer, 25, in Austin County, where they continued to live.

Wilhelm married Frederike Laas in late 1859 or early 1860, based on an Austin County marriage license dated December 28, 1859. Born June 26, 1840, she was approximately 12 years younger than Wilhelm, and the daughter of German immigrants Gottlieb and Frederike Laas.

No one with the surname "Kempe" appears in the 1860 census for Austin County, although there is a person identified as "F. Kemprg," 29, farmer, with wife "F." 18, with a mark indicating that they had married within the past year. Wilhelm's other given name, Friedrich, sometimes appears as his first name in early records. But he would have been 32 in 1860. Frederike would have been 20. On the other hand, census and other records of the 19th century often include significant errors in people's ages and the spelling of their names. As with any human endeavor, there are any number of reasons for this. Perhaps language barriers arose. Maybe people weren't cooperative with census takers, or maybe census takers were not particularly careful about accuracy. And probably census takers sometimes had to depend

Frederike Laas Kempe
1840-1895

on neighbors for information about a particular household, and those neighbors often could only approximate the ages and correct spelling of the absent family. That seems a good possibility here because the gap between the reported ages, as well as the reported ages themselves, is reasonably close to matching those of Wilhelm and Frederike.

Wilhelm and Frederike moved to neighboring Fayette County soon after their marriage. Baptismal records indicate that their first child was born there in 1861. Tax records in Fayette County indicate that Wilhelm owned land near Freyburg for the first time in 1866. He had 100 acres, worth $500 at the time, and not much else. No horses, mules, cattle, or miscellaneous property is reported in that first year, as it is in those following. Ten years later, he had twice that much land and horses and cattle.

The lives of Wilhelm and his family were severely affected by the Civil War in the 1860s. During the early part of the war, Wilhelm was able to remain home. But later he was away from his family and outside of Texas for an extended period. His role and activities – and which side he supported – remain unclear, as noted in more detail later in this book.

Wilhelm and his wife had nine children, but only six lived to adulthood. They were Auguste Emma "Emma" (born in 1861, died in 1942 at 81), who married Paul Grasshoff; Wilhelm Frederick (born in 1862, died in 1949 at 87), who married Helena Rabe; Herman Heinrich (born in 1864, died in 1935 at 71), who married Sophia Lockman; Amalie Dorothea (born in 1867, died in 1938 at 71), who married Henry Rudolph Thulemeyer; August Bernhard "Ben" (born in 1874, died in 1957 at 82), who married Maggie McGill; and Paul Alvin (born in 1876, died in 1938 at 62), who married Anna Kasper.

Twins Emilia (February 16, 1868-January 12, 1872) and Carl Edward (February 16, 1868-December 10, 1872) died as children at ages three and four. Daughter Henriette Bertha (September 24, 1870-November 9, 1882) died at age 12.

Wilhelm's wife Frederike was only 55 when she died on December 28, 1895. Following her death, Wilhelm lived first with his son Wilhelm Kempe Jr. and his family in Fayette County. Later, he lived with another son, Ben Kempe, and his family – first in Fayette County and then in Jim Wells County, Texas.

Wilhelm was 91 when he died on February 22, 1920 at Alice in Jim Wells County. He is buried next to his wife at Freyburg Methodist Cemetery, Freyburg, Fayette County, Texas.

Part II

War Between
the States

Chapter Two

GERMAN IMMIGRANTS
AND THE CIVIL WAR

As the slavery issue came to a head in the U.S., many German immigrants – especially those who had come to Texas more recently – supported abolition. They had no experience with slavery in their native land and tended to own smaller farms, which they could more easily work with their own families or hired help, compared to those of slave owners. So they generally had no desire or need for slaves. More than a few objected on moral grounds as well.

As a result, many German immigrants were pro-union and against secession of Texas from the U.S. The vote for secession failed by large margins in many Austin, Colorado, and Fayette county towns where German immigrants accounted for most of the population. For example, the vote was 8 for secession and 99 against at Cat Spring, 22 for and 154 against at Frelsburg, 10 for and 41 against at Dunlavy (area represented today by Mentz and Bernardo), and 7 for and 37 against at Harvey's Creek (represented today by Weimar).[6] Notably, some other nearby towns with heavy populations of German immigrants did favor secession by similar large margins, however. For example, the vote at Industry in Austin County was 86 for, 2 against. And secession was favored 36 to 30 at New Ulm, also in Austin County.[7] Secession won the day statewide as well, so Texas became part of the Confederacy.

After secession, many German immigrants who voted against it in Austin, Colorado, and Fayette counties resisted mandatory conscription, which became effective in April 1862. They held meetings, often

---

[6] Weyand, Leonie Rummel, and Wade, Houston. *An Early History of Fayette County.* (La Grange, Texas: La Grange Journal, 1936). 245

[7] Kamphoefner, Walter D. "New Perspectives on Texas Germans and the Confederacy." *Southwestern Historical Quarterly*, vol. CII, no. 4 (April 1999).

---

attended by hundreds, to discuss the issues and determine their next steps.[8]

In January 1863, a delegation representing the German immigrants of the area presented a declaration of resistance to the local Confederate brigadier general, William G. Webb. Their primary concern, according to the document, was that their families would suffer and be unprotected.

The proclamation stated that "the past has already taught us how regardlessly the Government and the county authorities have treated the families of those who have taken the field."

And, "Last year we made tolerably good crops; the prospect for the next is not very encouraging, and we cannot look forward with indifference upon starvation, which we apprehend for our wives and children."

Following later, "Besides the duty of defending one's country there is a higher and more sacred one – the duty of maintaining the families."

And unless the safety of their families could be guaranteed, "we shall not be able to answer the call, and the consequences must be attributed to those who caused them.

The declaration ended with even stronger words: "Furthermore, we decline taking the army oath (as prescribed) to the Confederate States, as we know of no law which compels Texas troops, who are designed for this state, to take the same."

It was signed by five men who said they acted in the name of about 120 citizens.[9]

In response, martial law to enforce the draft was declared in Austin, Colorado, and Fayette counties in January 1863.[10] Before the arrival of troops to enforce the measure, most of the Germans joined local militias, found other ways to legally serve the Confederacy, fled, or hid.

---

[8] Scott, Robert Nicholson. *The War of the Rebellion: A Compilation of the Official Records of the Union and Confederate Armies.* (U.S. War Department, published in Historical Times, 1886.) 925-928.

[9] Ibid. 928-929

[10] Ibid. 975

Chapter Three

LETTERS:
THE 1860s AND THE CIVIL WAR

Before draft resistance reached its peak in 1863, Wilhelm's brother-in-law, John Mayer, had joined a Confederate unit. Mayer was enrolled as a private in Captain Robert Voigt's Company, Waul's Texas Legion, on a June 15, 1862 muster roll at Camp Waul, which was about seven miles north of Brenham, in Washington County. For July and August 1862, he was a private in Company E, 1 Infantry Battalion, Waul's Texas Legion. For September and October, he was in Company C of the same battalion, and he was listed as sick in September. His illness continued in November and December, when he was absent and listed as sick on muster rolls. By order of a Dr. Randall on December 16, 1862, he was sent to a hospital.

Later, Mayer was one of tens of thousands of Confederate soldiers captured by Union forces with the fall of Vicksburg on July 4, 1863. He was paroled – allowed to return home if he pledged not to take up arms against Union forces until he could be formally exchanged for Union prisoners[11] – on July 17, 1863, a mere two weeks later.

An August 10, 1863 letter written to Wilhelm by Auguste Kempe Mayer, who is Mayer's wife and Wilhelm's sister, indicates that Mayer has not returned to his home near New Ulm in Austin County, but is expected soon. Auguste notes that Mayer suffered a gunshot wound to his leg.

Auguste seems troubled and wants to move for reasons left undisclosed in the letter, but she also writes that she and her children live in peace, according to the translated text. Perhaps an error in the original

---

[11] Formal prisoner exchanges were codified by the U.S. and the Confederacy in July 1862. The U.S. suspended its participation in the formal system in May 1863, although individual military leaders continued exchanges until early 1864, when the practice was banned. After the confederacy agreed to a one-to-one exchange rate for Black soldiers of equivalent rank and remedied other irregularities, the U.S. renewed its participation in early 1865. Soldiers were paroled, rather than exchanged, when one side had prisoners remaining after the other side had offered all of its prisoners.

---

translation could have altered slightly the meaning of some of the words, thereby producing this apparent inconsistency.

She also mentions that she is "going on in years." She's only 29, but probably feels much older from the stress of the war.

Auguste's letter further suggests that Wilhelm has had some unidentified troubles of his own, and that he has been able to stay home, but might soon have to leave. Unfortunately, there is no other hint as to what troubles he had, why he remains home, why he might have to leave, or what he might have to do.

Auguste's letter also refers to now-unknown people and places – "Rius," "Ruehn," and "Nertliezen" – names which could have been misinterpreted by the original translator in the 1960s. Their significance to the lives of the Kempes in Texas remains unexplained.

On a happier note at the end of her letter, Auguste offers good wishes "from Emma to your Emma." She refers to her daughter, 5 at the time, and Wilhelm's daughter, 2, who shared that given name.

1. Auguste to Wilhelm – August 10, 1863, from New Ulm [Texas]

Dear Brother and Sister-in-Law,

Your letter dated July 23 I received August 9. I can see that all of you are doing fine except you. I am very sorry to hear that but I am glad you could stay home. We are all doing fine.

Dear brother, with the moving I just wait and see until he is here. I expect him every day now. He was wounded on the leg and had to stay in the hospital. The bullet went through his leg but ruined the bone. Three of the Rius live here now but the fourth one stayed on in Nertliezen. When Rius left, Ludwig Ruehn told me that his leg was much better and that he soon would be able to leave.

Dear Brother and Sister-in-Law I just cannot tell you in what peace my children and I live. And when he comes and his leg will not hinder him we will drive up there right away. Because when I tell him what all happened to me here, he also wants to move. When I told the people here that I want to move they told me I was wrong, that I was going on in years and that I should keep the farm.

*If you have to leave, write me another letter so I know
when you have to go.
A greeting from Emma to your Emma.
Many greetings to you, your wife and children,*

Your loving sister,
Auguste Mayer

Wilhelm's role in the Civil War is difficult to pinpoint with any certainty. Letters and other documents offer clues, but many of them appear inconsistent and puzzling.

No doubt the war and the strong political emotions leading up to it dashed Wilhelm's early hopes of living the American Dream – the opportunity to live a life of free choice, with opportunities to apply skills and hard work to build a bright future. It's not difficult to imagine that he and other relatively recent German immigrants had no particular strong feelings for either the North or the South, but merely wanted to be left alone to pursue their personal goals, building their adopted country in that way. For many of them, decisions about how to cope with the war must have been difficult. Perhaps that is why the Civil War role of Wilhelm F. Kempe, the 1854 immigrant from Saxony, is unclear.

By early 1861, about a year after their marriage, Wilhelm and Frederike had moved from Austin County to the Pin Oak area of southwestern Fayette County, where their first child was born in February 1861.

Their second and third children were born in June 1862 and March 1864, indicating that he must have been with his family – at least periodically – as late as summer 1863. The August 10, 1863 letter (see previous) from his sister Auguste also suggests that she believes that he is at home then.

His presence at home as late as summer 1863 is curious. Wilhelm was 35 at the time and subject to conscription since the maximum draft age was increased from 35 to 45 the previous year. Also, martial law to enforce the draft in Austin, Colorado, and Fayette counties had been in place since January. Wilhelm would have been expected to become a

Confederate solider, but his name has not been found in enlistment re-cords.[12]

The evidence is clear, however, that for some reason Wilhelm did leave home for an extended period just before or within the 12 months following the August 1863 letter from Auguste that places him there. Writing to his family from St. Louis in November 1864, he mentions being in New Orleans in August, in St. Louis in September, in Illinois as snowfall began that fall, and in St. Louis again in November.

All of these places were under Union control when the letter was written. New Orleans was captured by Union forces in April 1862 and held for the rest of the war. St. Louis was under Union control, more or less, for the entire war, and Confederate forces didn't invade Illinois. Also, there were no normal postal connections from St. Louis to Texas in 1864, so possibly the letter was delivered by a friend or some kind of courier.[13]

Wilhelm wishes to return home, he writes, but there's a strong im-plication that he's unable to do so. He also mentions working on a farm while in Illinois, indicating that he must not have been a front-line sol-dier at the time. These clues led to speculation by some of his descen-dants that he was a Confederate solider held prisoner by Union forces.

A piece of family hearsay supports this theory. As recorded in a single sentence in a 1960s-era, one-page family history, one of Wilhelm's granddaughters told others of a childhood memory of her grandfather in possession of a document with the word "amnesty" writ-

---

[12] A search of enlistment records for Confederate forces in Texas seems to offer two possibilities – a Private William "Kempe" and a Private William "Kampe." Careful examination suggests that these records represent the same person whose name was spelled either "Kempe" or "Kampe" and even "Campe" in different parts of his record. But this soldier was not Wilhelm F. Kempe, the 1854 immigrant from Sayda in Saxony. The soldier's records indicate that he was 26 in 1861, that his enlistment period began in June 1861, and that he was a musician. Wilhelm would have turned 33 in 1861, was certainly at home in fall 1861 when his second child was conceived, and left no evi-dence that he was ever a musician of any kind. Also, the soldier signed his name as "Wm. Kampe" (not "Kempe") on the document that secured his parole and release from captivity.

[13] Kamphoefner, Walter D. "Civil War." Email to Ray Grasshoff. September 1, 2000. "It's a little puzzling as to how the mail would even get through from St. Louis to Texas in 1864; there weren't any normal postal connections." Indeed, the U.S. and the Confederacy ceased mail interchange on June 1, 1861.

ten on it.[14] During and at the end of the Civil War, the U.S. Congress passed official acts offering amnesty to Confederate soldiers who would pledge allegiance to the U.S.

But studies of various lists of Confederate prisoners find only a single reference to someone with the same or similar name. Prisoner "Kempe, Wm." – who might be the same Kempe/Kampe soldier/musician referenced previously in footnote 12 – received a letter and $25 in February 1865 at the Union's Point Lookout prison camp in Maryland. Although the camp held some Confederate soldiers from Texas, there is no other indication that Wilhelm was that far away from Texas at any point.

Still other evidence – or more precisely, the lack of evidence – suggests that Wilhelm was not a Confederate soldier. The Kempe name is not on the list of Civil War indigent families in Fayette County, where Frederike and the children still lived when Wilhelm was away.[15] These lists were created after the Texas Legislature in December 1863 passed a law setting aside funds for the "families, widows, and dependents of soldiers currently serving in State or Confederate forces." Many, if not all, of the families of Confederate soldiers from the area appear on the list.

Other evidence suggests that Wilhelm perhaps did not support the Confederate cause, but was instead supporting the Union effort in some way. His reference to working on a farm in Illinois seems to back this argument. Almost invariably, others' accounts of life in Civil War prison camps – both Union and Confederate – describe a miserable existence with no suggestion that prisoners ever set foot outside the prison walls, much less work on a farm. That would have been an extremely unlikely activity for a captured Confederate soldier.

Perhaps other clues to Wilhelm's role are contained in the undated cover note that accompanied his November 1, 1864 letter from St. Louis. Wilhelm wrote the letter to his wife Frederike, but he did not

---

[14] "Historian's Report." Unpublished report prepared for a Kempe family reunion in an unknown year. Date unknown. Author unknown.

[15] Wilhelm and his family lived in Fayette County by early 1861 and throughout the Civil War and beyond, based on the place of birth noted for his children in their church baptismal records and subsequent tax and census records. A reference to "Kemper, 3" in 1864, and "Mrs. Kemper, 3" in April 1865 on the list of indigent families in Austin County refers to another family. Since names were frequently misspelled in these types of records, this item once brought interest as a possible reference to the Kempe family.

send it directly to her. Instead, he sent it to his sister Auguste, asking her in the cover note to forward the letter to Frederike. Wilhelm's request might suggest the need for a deceptive route to communicate with his wife. Possibly he wished to keep others in the area from knowing his whereabouts, or that his wife had received a letter from him, which is plausible if he was indeed supporting the Union effort in some way.

On the other hand, in the absence of regular mail service between the U.S. and the Confederacy, perhaps someone who had contact with Wilhelm merely delivered the messages to Auguste so that she could pass them on to Frederike.

Another less intriguing possibility is that Wilhelm at the time also wrote a letter to his sister, and that he merely included both in the same package. But that seems unlikely, since the cover note itself contains a few heartfelt words directed to Auguste, suggesting that there was not another simultaneous communication to her.

In the cover note, Wilhelm tells Auguste that he wants to leave the U.S. and return to Germany – a thought he never expressed in any other existing note or letter. His feelings are palpable, if only noted in a single line, and a good indication of how the Civil War years affected the lives of new immigrants.

The cover note offers still other intriguing, if indirect, clues to Wilhelm's activities. He refers to a "Dr. Nagel," most probably meaning Dr. Herman Nagel, who in the 1850s had moved to Texas intending to farm rather than practice medicine. But his professional services were vitally needed in rural Texas, and he provided them in Austin County.

Dr. Nagel supported the Union and decided to flee Texas in November 1863. Leaving his wife and two children behind, he and a son[16] went to Mexico, took a ship to New York, and made their way to St.

---

[16] Charles Nagel, the son who fled Texas with his father, documented that and related events in *A Boy's Civil War Story*, published in 1934. Born August 9, 1849 in Colorado County, Charles became a lawyer in his new home state of Missouri. Later, he served in the Missouri House of Representatives, as president of the St. Louis City Council, and as a member of the Republican National Committee. In 1909, U.S. President William Howard Taft appointed him U.S. Secretary of Commerce and Labor. His first wife, Fannie Brandeis, was the sister of U.S. Supreme Court Justice Louis Brandeis. Nagel's second wife was the mother of their son Charles Jr., who became director of several major art museums, including the National Portrait Gallery of the Smithsonian Institution.

Louis. He re-established his medical practice there. A year later, his wife – also traveling through Mexico and New York – joined him. Tragically, death had taken the two children who had stayed in Texas with her.

Wilhelm's connection to Dr. Nagel is unclear, but the reference to him suggests that they were acquainted. Perhaps they shared the same views.

The Nagel story might also explain the significance of Wilhelm's particular reference to "what happened in Brownsville" in the letter to his wife. Brownsville is at the southern tip of Texas and a gateway to Mexico. After Union forces blockaded ports in the South, much of the Confederacy's cotton crop was shipped to Europe through the city. In November 1863 – at the same time Dr. Nagel fled to Mexico – Union troops attacked, forcing Confederate forces to withdraw. In July 1864, Confederate forces retook the town. Wilhelm's apparent reference to the reoccupation is intriguing and suggests that it has some significance for him and his wife. Some German immigrants served the Confederacy by transporting cotton to Brownsville, and then returning with needed supplies. Perhaps he became such a cotton teamster, crossed the border into Mexico on a journey south, and then boarded a ship to New Orleans and then up the Mississippi to St. Louis and Illinois.[17] Such a scenario was not unheard of among Fayette County men.[18]

Soon after the end of the war, Wilhelm returned home to his family in Texas, receiving no apparent retribution from others for his wartime activities, as might have been expected if he fled Texas to avoid any type of military service.

Taken together, the evidence discovered to date fails to clearly define the nature of Wilhelm's activities during the Civil War. Some of it points to support for the Confederate cause, while some of it suggests support for the Union cause. Possibly he played both sides.

---

[17] Kamphoefner, Walter D. "Civil War" email to Ray Grasshoff. Wilhelm "might have gone to Brownsville as a cotton teamster and slipped across the border there, then caught a ship to New Orleans and a boat up the river." There's also the "slight possibility" that Wilhelm "took the oath to the Union and swore off the Confederacy after being captured, as some of the Waul's Legion Germans did. However, in that case he would have been inducted into the Union army and sent to serve somewhere on the Indian frontier."

[18] Weyand and Wade. *Early History of Fayette County*, 259.

On another issue, the man and woman referenced in the letter as "C.O." and his wife remain unidentified. Misinterpretation of the original German script for these initials is possible.

2. Wilhelm to Auguste – [undated, but presumed November 1, 1864, from St. Louis]

Dearest Sister!

Please be so good and send this letter to my wife. I know you will do it or I would not bother you with it. I do not know whether your husband is home or not but I wish with all my heart that he can be with his family. And that this letter will reach you all doing well.

Oh dear sister, do I wish that we all could go back to our German Fatherland and escape this hopeless future. Please dear sister, also send the letter from Dr. Nagel's wife to my wife. Perhaps this would be a good way to exchange letters.

Hope you are all doing all right, this is my honest wish.

W. K.

3. Wilhelm to Frederike – November 1, 1864, from St. Louis

My beloved Frederike!

Again I will write you with a sad heart to tell you about me and where I am. I hope to God that my letter will reach you, the children and your father doing all right.

Thank goodness we are still well. That is my biggest wish that God will keep us healthy and let us have our daily bread and bless and keep us. For two months we were in the state of Illinois and worked on a farm. But soon it was too cold and then snow fell, so we had to go back to St. Louis to find work. My dearest, believe me I do not like it any place, I have no peace and the thought of my family in Texas breaks my heart. Especially when I see happy children with their father and mother I could cry but I am a man and have to take it. After all, in a war men also have to leave their family and are even in danger every hour of the day. So my beloved wife we just have to have patience and be brave and pray that everything will turn out all right.

I am sure you heard what happened in Brownsville and I also sent you a letter from New Orleans, dated August 6, and one from St. Louis dated September 1. Of course, whether you received my letters I do not know but I do hope so with all my heart.

I wish I could find out how all of you are doing. Please, dear, stay close to my sister, write her often. You have a good friend in her. Whether we are doing the right thing now, and whether it will be our good luck or bad luck we just have to see.

Dear wife, tell C.O.'s wife many greetings. He feels just as I do and is just as unhappy as I.

God keep all of you, this I wish with all my heart.

Your true and forever loving husband,
W. K.

Part III

Fatherland

Chapter Four

LETTERS:
THE 1870s AND GERMANY

The 1860s also brought war to Wilhelm's native Saxony. The kingdom had been part of the German Confederation since that union was created after Napoleon's defeat in 1815. Two other members of the confederation – the Kingdom of Prussia and the Austrian Empire – were the dominant members and became rivals for supremacy. War broke out between those two powers in 1866, and Saxony supported the Austrians. Prussia's victory later that year resulted in the creation in 1867 of the North German Confederation, which included Saxony but excluded Austria.

This Austro-Prussian War (also known as the Seven Weeks War) and its consequences meant changes for Wilhelm's family back in Saxony. Hints to those changes are offered in what remains of a letter to Wilhelm from his father August Friedrich Kempe. The first part of the letter is missing, so it is undated. But the remaining part of the letter refers to a storm in December 1868, suggesting that the letter was probably written in 1869. Based on that reasoning, the Austro-Prussian War must be the conflict that it references.

In his letter, August reports that his taxes have increased as a result of the war, and that Wilhelm's younger brother Alwin, who was about 23, is a soldier. But more than anything, August mourns the loss of Wilhelm to Texas, and is not shy about expressing his feelings.

Saxony and other German lands lost many of their best and brightest young people to the adventure of a new, more promising life in a new land across the ocean. Much of the early German emigration, in the 1830s and 1840s, was generated by glowing reports of life and resources in Texas.[19] Johann Friedrich Ernst, recognized as the first German immigrant to Texas and founder of the town of Industry in Austin

---

[19] Schünemann, C. *The Emigrant to Texas: A Handbook & Guide*. Bremen, Germany, 1846. Translated by Otto W. Tetzlaff. Burnet, Texas. Eakin Publications, ca.1979

County, was especially influential with letters that were published in Germany. Soon the Adelsverein, an organization created by a group of German noblemen to facilitate mass emigration of Germans for colonization in Texas, became the biggest player in the effort. The noblemen hoped that German settlements in Texas would give German industry additional markets and help develop German maritime commerce. Before the underfunded Adelsverein went bankrupt in 1853, it brought thousands of Germans to Texas and no doubt planted the idea in the minds of many more.[20]

In addition to those and other promotional efforts, poor harvests from German farms in 1846 and 1847 made even more Germans look for a better place to live. Those poor agricultural yields also helped stoke political unrest throughout the German Confederation.

Soon those political strains became another factor. Encouraged by the abdication of the French king in early 1848, a new liberalism arose in the German states. Followers sought reforms that would guarantee representative government, freedom of the press, and other democratic measures. The unrest reached its head with widespread mass protests later that year. By the end of 1848, the revolution had fizzled, and German monarchs retained their autocratic rule. As a result, many well-educated Germans joined others in leaving their homeland for a new life in Texas and other parts of the U.S. in the 1850s.

War, economic turmoil, and political unrest offer only very general clues about why many Germans left their homeland. But how much of a factor were they in the decisions of Wilhelm Kempe and his sister to leave Sayda with little desire to ever return? What other factors might have played a role?

By emigrating, Wilhelm turned his back on what seemed to have been a solid future in Sayda. The Kempes had a strong family history in the area, where they had lived for generations. Wilhelm's father was a successful farmer and landowner. Although probably not rich, he was not poor, based on his ability to seek and obtain medical care and surgery in the city. He seemed to welcome the opportunity to pass on his holdings to a responsible heir.

Did Wilhelm leave to avoid a future in farming? If so, there were better choices than rural, undeveloped Texas in the mid-19th century.

---

[20] Brister, Louis B. "Adelsverein." *The Handbook of Texas Online*, February 28, 2009. <http://www.tshaonline.org/handbook/online/articles/AA/ufa1.html>

Or did he have other expectations, based on the glowing reports of Texas from the Adelsverein and other similar promotional efforts?

Perhaps the few existing notes of Wilhelm's journal and the Kempe letters offer a few hints. The earliest entry in what's left of the journal is dated 1852, two years before Wilhelm left for Texas. So he had already left home and was traveling, perhaps indicating a youthful desire to see and meet new people and see new places as a young adult of 24. Possibly reading Adelsverein reports of great opportunities for a bright future in Texas, he made that his goal.

Other factors might have played a role, too. Many of the Kempe letters offer insights into the possibly frustrating personality and demeanor of his widowed father, August Kempe. Perhaps those qualities, especially when endured in the absence of a mother to moderate them and provide a balance, made life in Sayda less desirable for Wilhelm and Auguste. There are severe limitations to the quality of personality insights gathered so indirectly, but the decades covered by the letters allow some consistent observations over a considerable length of time. Through the years, August Kempe seems highly manipulative, annoyingly stubborn, and accepting of only events and activities that meet his strict expectations. To be fair, possibly that is all that can be expected from an aging man who has lost most of his family to premature death and still others to personal choices such as emigration. But it is not hard to imagine a difficult life with him.

In this first letter from August, who is about 70, he is heartbroken by Wilhelm's absence, although 15 years have passed since the son left for Texas. August dreams of visiting Texas and asks Wilhelm to send photos of his family. He begs him to write more often, and notes that he has not received a letter sent from his son-in-law, John Mayer, in Texas. The absence of letters from Wilhelm could be attributed to blockade of Confederate ports during the Civil War. Mail-carrying ships could not leave.

August also asks Wilhelm to write to his Aunt Weigel in Dresden, the capital of Saxony. She is Amalie Kempe Weigel, August's younger sister and the mother of Wilhelm's Weigel cousins, with whom he will exchange many letters in coming years.

The full identity of the "Mr. Wiegand" and the "cousin Treisler" mentioned by August remain unknown.

4. August to Wilhelm and Frederike – [undated, but ca. 1869, from Sayda]

[Only last part of this translated letter survives.]

Because of the war we have a new law which requires us to pay more taxes which hit me pretty hard. Last year while we had the church bazaar, Alwin visited us for eight days. He looked fine and was happy and the soldier life does not seem to bother him. And as long as we can live in peace it is not so hard to be a soldier.

Dear Wilhelm, almost daily I write in my big book which I am sure you still can remember. I wish you could read it, I am sure you would be interested in it.

I wish I could visit you once, then my biggest wish would be fulfilled and if I could be younger I would do it and would not care how much money I had to spend, because my longing for my children gets bigger and bigger. I regret so much that I ever let you go and to think I should die without having seen you again makes my heart heavy.

That is why I ask you, dear Wilhelm, please write me more often and let me know all about you and how you are doing. You wrote that my son-in-law wrote me last year. I never received his letter or I would have answered it long ago. I was so afraid that you did not receive my last letter or that I wrote a wrong address. You know it was almost two years that I was without a letter from you so please don't let me wait again that long and write me once or twice every year. I also have a wish, that if possible, you would send me a photograph from your wife. I do enjoy so much looking at your photograph. I shall send you many greetings from your cousin Treisler from [Alberulzan?]; he has a lumber company. And please send greetings to Mr. Barthol; he is always so interested in your letters and we always sit together in the evenings and talk about you. Also write once to your Aunt Weigel in Dresden. I sent her your letter to read. Also let me know if Mr. Wiegand wrote you; he told Bertha that he would do so.

You don't know what beautiful weather we have now. All of the snow is gone and it is so warm and sunny. Also, we had a terrible storm on December 7, 1868. We were terri-

fied as houses and churches and many trees were torn down. They estimated damage at four million.

That is all the news I know and so I hope that you will write me soon again. Please let my son-in-law read this letter too. With many greetings.

Your loving father and father-in-law,
A. F. Kempe

In Europe, another war soon followed the Austro-Prussian War. This time, Prussia and its North German Confederation allies took on France.

Prussia and other German states had maintained a grudge against France since Napoleon's army ravaged them before his defeat in 1815. Most historians seem to agree that Prussian statesman Otto von Bismarck capitalized on this resentment to engineer a war with France and thereby further unify the German states through a fight against a common enemy.

At the same time, France's Napoleon III, stung by years of reverses in its efforts to maintain its leading role among European nations, also itched for battle to secure his country's prestige.

The Franco-Prussian War began in summer 1870 and ended in spring 1871 with Prussian victory. Success on the battlefield stoked widespread German nationalism, playing into Bismarck's unification plans.

In early 1871, Prussian King Wilhelm I became head of the united German states, known as the German Empire until 1918, when Wilhelm II abdicated the throne as Germany was defeated in World War I.

In an August 1870 letter to Wilhelm, August notes the war and that Wilhelm's brother Alwin is a soldier who is probably fighting on the front. August awaits word that Alwin, his only remaining son in Germany after Wilhelm's departure, has survived battle. August adds that he is enclosing a letter Alwin wrote to Wilhelm about six weeks prior.

It's not surprising that August, who hasn't seen Wilhelm in 16 years and has never seen his son's wife and family, continues to ask for photographs of them. By 1870, a few photographers had established permanent businesses in some small cities, such as La Grange in neighboring Fayette County, so photos were possible. Wilhelm's sister Auguste Kempe Mayer – known to close family members as "Gustel" –

has made the effort. August is overjoyed to have received photos of her family, whom he has also never seen.

This letter is also notable since it indicates that German immigrants in Texas – even those without fiscal connections to the Adelsverein and other formal colonization organizations – were seeking others to join them. August reports that he has not found appropriate people to meet a request from his son-in-law, John Mayer, in Texas. As unhappy as August remains about the decision of his son and daughter to emigrate, it's hard to believe that he would seriously help recruit others from Sayda.

5. August and Bertha to Wilhelm and Auguste – August 28, 1870, from Sayda

My Dearest Children,

I do hope very much that this letter will reach you safely, as I am worried since you wrote that you are wondering why I am not writing you. I wrote you a long letter with many important matters and also asked you several questions to answer me right away. I even put two pictures of Alwin in it, which are lost now. Please answer this short letter right away, then I will write you again as I still have to tell you many things.

As you perhaps read in your newspaper already, we do have another one of those terrible wars. Since France declared war on Prussia and Saxony belongs to the North German Confederation, our men have to go to war too. And also our Alwin. He had to leave six weeks ago and now we are ever so worried whether he is well and if he will come back to us or not. He wrote us once on August 10 but now there have been terrible battles and we have not heard from him. He also wrote you a letter the last day he was at home, which I send you with this letter.

On July 15, 1870, I received a letter from my son-in-law and Gustel [Auguste] and I was very happy as there were six pictures in it with all the children. I had them framed right away and put them on the wall and now I am so happy every time I look at my grandchildren. My biggest

wish is to see them once in person. I also would love to have a picture of you and my dear daughter-in-law, so please if you can have one made and send it to us.

Gustel sent Bertha a gold coin and was Bertha ever excited and happy about it.

Please let Mayers know about it and tell them I will write them as soon as I know that you received this letter.

My son-in-law also wrote me if I could not find some men which would come over to live but I could not find anyone yet, and they also had to be good and trustworthy people. But I doubt that I will find them now, but keep trying. In the next letter I will put some more pictures of Alwin, hoping that they will reach you then.

Please always write your address very clear on your letter, then I know that I am sending my letter to the right address.

Thank goodness my health is good, only my legs are getting old. Bertha also is doing fine, and she is going to write a letter to Gustel to say her thanks. I will close my letter now with the hope to hear from you again. And that all of you are doing well.

Many hearty greetings,
With many good wishes,
Bertha Kempe (and) your loving father Kempe

Alwin was 24 when he faced war again as a soldier in 1870. Visiting Sayda before leaving to join the fight, he writes a short letter to his brother and sister in Texas. Only eight when his older siblings left for Texas 16 years ago, his occasional short notes to them suggest that he understandably feels little familial connection. This letter provides only an impersonal account of current events, the duty that calls him, and his hope to come through battle intact.

In a postscript, Alwin sends greetings from the Weigel family – an aunt, uncle, and cousins. Several of the Weigel cousins will send their own letters to Wilhelm in coming years.

Several errors were obvious in the original translation of this letter from Alwin. Most seriously, the translation dated it in 1871, not 1870. But the information provided by Alwin indicates clearly that it was written as the Franco-Prussian War began. That war ended in the first part of 1871, and Prussia did not engage France in a subsequent war later in the year. The original translation also had "Russia," not Prussia, declaring war on France. Russia remained neutral in the conflict.

Alwin also is not entirely correct when he says that Denmark has also declared war on Prussia. Although Denmark had also suffered setbacks in territorial disputes with Prussia and therefore favored France, the Danish government did not formally enter the war.

6. Alwin to Wilhelm and Frederike, John and Auguste – July 20, 1870, from Sayda

> *My Dear Honored Brother, Sister,*
> *Brother-in-Law and Sister-in-Law,*
>
> *So long I wanted to write but always something happened and I hope you forgive me. It is sad news I have to write you but we have the whole country in unrest again. France and Denmark declared war on Prussia and since our state belongs to the North German Confederation we are included. [Prussia] also declared war on France.*
> *So now every young man from 20 to 32 years of age has to be a soldier and since I was in military duty before I have to be in Dresden on July 22 and again fight for my Fatherland, and perhaps die with a bullet for it. I came here to say goodbye to our father and sister and are very homesick for you.*
> *But I am so happy that you seem to be doing well. Father told me that you did not receive the last letter which is a pity because I had two pictures of me in it.*
> *Dear Brother and relatives I am happy now, since I have to go to battle again, I wrote you once again and hope it will not be my last letter to you.*
>
>
>
> *With all my love,*
> *Your loving brother and brother-in-law,*
> *Alwin Kempe*
>
>
> *Many greetings from the whole family Weigel.*

Premature death was no stranger to the Kempe family. Of the 11 children born to August and Christiane Hoepfner Kempe in Saxony, only four – Wilhelm, his brother Alwin, and his sisters Auguste and Bertha – lived to be adults. Their mother Christiane died at 40, only a few months after giving birth to Alwin.

Still, news from Texas of Auguste's death at 36 was shocking to her father August and sister Bertha in Europe. In separate letters to Wilhelm, they mourn her loss with expressions of deep grief, even though they haven't seen her in nearly 17 years.

The precise date of her death is forgotten and apparently unrecorded, and searches for her grave have been fruitless. Auguste was alive as late as September 13, 1870, the date on which a census taker recorded her as the wife of John Mayer in Austin County.[21] She must have died later that year, since August and Bertha received the news from Texas prior to writing their January letters in response.

The cause of Auguste's death is now forgotten and unrecorded as well. Yellow fever was a common scourge in the 1800s, and epidemics were common every few years. For example, an 1867 epidemic in nearby La Grange brought reports of unmarked mass burials in trenches at the site of the town's present cemetery.[22]Although there are no reports of such an epidemic in 1870, the disease was common during the period.

Auguste lingered on her deathbed long enough to ask that Bertha come to Texas to mother her four daughters. Bertha writes Wilhelm that she cannot tear herself away from her duty to take care of their aging father, whose hopes for the future now depend on youngest son Alwin returning home from the army to take over the family farm.

---

[21] Williams, Velmalene. Letter and information to Ray Grasshoff. January 19, 2006. Auguste and husband John Mayer had four daughters: Emma (born January 18, 1858 at New Ulm, Austin County, Texas, and married Charlie Brackenbusch, and then his brother Henry W. Brackenbusch after Charlie's death); Bertha (born July 29, 1861 in New Ulm, Austin County, Texas, and married Heinrich Gustave Backhaus); Mary Margaret (born September 18, 1864 in New Ulm, Austin County, Texas, and married Henry Schmiedekamp); and Anna (born August 4, 1868 in New Ulm, Austin County, Texas, and married Michael Feist). John Mayer and his daughters moved to Milam County, Texas in 1873, according to the obituary of Bertha Mayer Backhaus.

[22] Ramos, Mary G. "The Deadly Visitor; Yellow Fever." *Texas Almanac*. February 28, 2009. <http://www.texasalmanac.com/history/highlights/fever/>

Bertha, nearly 27, also writes that she has strong feelings for a man she has been seeing, but is afraid of the commitment required for marriage. Even after living with her father and his oppressive tendencies, she fears losing her independence as a married woman.

7. Bertha to Wilhelm – January 18, 1871, from Sayda

My Dear Beloved Brother!

With deep mourning in my heart, I take the pen to write a little letter to you, my beloved brother in a distant country, alas, only to you; it is not anymore granted to me to write a few words to my sister. Oh, the terrible news has cut a deep wound into our hearts, we are inconsolable about the loss of our dear Gustel [Auguste]. *I can't describe the moment to you when we received your letter and when I should read the terrible words to father, who was so curious, and wanted to listen to me so full of hope, but alas, oh disgrace, already during the first words my voice started to tremble, the terrible word did not want to pass my tongue, I was not able to continue reading, I had to cry loudly and father joined me – we did not believe it was possible, again and again we looked at the letter, but it did not change, oh the loving and deeply hurt heart wants to cry out, full of despair. Oh, God, why did you do this! But God's wisdom is too dark and too hidden for us to discern why he could let this happen, here man reaches the limit, where all knowledge, all research finds its end, where only faith, men's only anchor for salvation, can be put in its place, where we have to rise our eyes to heaven, where He dwells, who rules according to His wisdom and will. He distributes ... and suffering ... who blesses, but also cuts the deepest wounds; indeed the pain is only too big when such a sweet and dear being has to be let go by its loved ones.*
Don't think, my dear brother, that just because we live far apart and don't know each other very well (as we only were little children when you separated from us), we don't feel the pain as strongly as if we had been together – oh, certainly the feelings and emotions are the same if we

were close together. You cannot imagine how many tears I already cried over the dear Gustel, how glad I am to be here and alone, so that I can dwell in my emotions and cry as much as I want, oh, how touched am I by those words that our beloved Gustel spoke on her deathbed, that she remembered me so dearly and even gave me with the holy obligation to become a mother to her motherless children, oh, how much I would like to fulfill your wish, my life depends on it, I want to leave my homeland right away to come to you and to the dear children, but alas, the duties of a daughter keep me here as it would be incredibly hard on me to leave father, and to persuade him to move together with me would also be very hard, should he still go on this long journey at his age and should he leave house and home then this would be very hard on him as he always was hoping that one day a child would continue the business, which naturally is not meant for me, however so much more for Alwin, if he just would return safely from the war, our fears and apprehension for him are great, news from the war makes us anxious and we urgently wait for letters from him, but so far God the Almighty has protected him and kept him well.

Dearest brother, I can tell you that so far I am still totally free and uncommitted, however I don't know how much longer, I have to admit that the heart is not completely free anymore, that I have had an acquaintanceship for awhile, which I already told you a couple of times, but I have not let myself become too committed yet and am thus still free to do what I want, I will also have a hard time to decide to get married, I imagine it being horrible, that is such an important step and thus I will wait a little bit longer, although I am not the youngest anymore I will continue to enjoy the worry-free with father for a little bit longer.

Beloved brother, I have allowed myself to include a note for our brother-in-law, please pass it on to him. Finally, please write us again right away, so that we know if you got our letter and the picture. Oh, how glad we are that we have Gustel's picture, we look at it often. It now has

twice the value for us; we also would like to get the pic-
ture of your dear wife and of the children.

Now goodbye my dear Wilhelm, stay healthy together
with your family and give my best regards to your dear
wife and the children, especially I greet you ...

Your sister Bertha

In addition to mourning Auguste, August fears for Alwin in the raging Franco-Prussian War. But even as he writes his letter, the war is winding down. An armistice will be signed only 10 days later – on January 28, 1871.

August also has news of his sister's family, the Weigels. Edward, their oldest son, has died unexpectedly. And Hermann, their only other son, has a chance meeting with Alwin on a battlefield.

Bertha, August notes, wants to visit Wilhelm in Texas. But August writes that he isn't up to the trip. No doubt he doesn't want Bertha to travel alone, for fear that she might not return and that he would lose another child to Texas.

For the first time, August also mentions his failing vision, an issue that becomes a major concern in the future.

8. August to Wilhelm – January 18, 1871, from Sayda

My good, dear son!

Received both of your sad letters. It was such a shock
and hurt for us and we could not help crying. I still cannot
believe that my Gustel [Auguste] is dead. We are always
so happy to receive mail from you and so Bertha opened
the letters fast to read them to me as my eyes are too weak
to read them myself, and then we heard the terrible news.
I don't know why the good Lord has given me such sorrow
in my old age even so I had many a hard time in my life.
But I had hoped so for peace in my few remaining years.

I also worry so much about Alwin. Today we received a
letter from him saying that he was doing fine and is
healthy. But he has enough of these wild times and wishes

he could come home soon. He is stationed near Paris and was in many battles and in great danger. He wrote that there was much death on both sides and that he lost many of his comrades. Such a terrible war Europe never had seen before. On the beginning of the war, Alwin and the others had almost nothing to eat so we sent him packages with food, also tobacco and a pipe. But now he wrote to stop sending them as he cannot carry it with him. It is also so terribly cold and many soldiers are sick and have parts of their bodies frozen. All hospitals are crowded with wounded and sick soldiers and Saxony alone has 50,000 French prisoners of war. On January 10, 8,000 men were drafted here again and they soon will go to France.

Dear Wilhelm, please visit your brother-in-law often and help him where you can. Also tell him to write to me and show him this letter. I am sorry that you two live so far apart; otherwise you could visit each other more often. It also made us sad to hear that you could not attend our Gustel's funeral.

I suppose you don't know that Edward Weigel died of tuberculosis at the hospital in Chemnitz. He was not married and worked too hard on his music. Everybody liked and honored him. He had saved over 1,000 Thaler[23] when he died. I wrote you that in the letter that was lost.

Hermann is also in the war with the Cavalry and he and Alwin met each other after one of the battles was over and were they ever surprised and happy to see that they both were still healthy and alive.

Dear son, you don't know how worried we are about Gustel's children. If it would be possible we would take a few of them and raise them. This way it would not be so

---

[23] The Thaler is a silver coin of different denominations and issued by various governments in Europe for hundreds of years, beginning about 1500. With the unification of Germany in the 1870s, the Mark became the major monetary unit for money among the unified states. But references to the Thaler much later in these letters indicate that it remained in use in some form. No effort to determine equivalent values between the Thaler and the U.S. dollar in the 19th century has been attempted here because such a study would appear to be difficult and subject to wide misinterpretation based on the different economies of the two nations. Notably, however, the term "dollar" derives from the term "Thaler."

hard on my son-in-law and you know that Bertha and I love children and would do everything for them.

I wish we would not live so far apart. We could come and visit you. Bertha keeps talking about it, but I am an old man and cannot make such a hard trip any more, even so I am longing to see you. Besides Bertha and I cannot leave here as Alwin had to finish his 12-year military service and then he will need my advice and help badly when he takes over the farm. I pray the good Lord will let me live a few more years. It would hurt me terrible if our property would go to strangers since I always kept it up so well. Even so, the taxes are hard and I do not want to sell any part of it. If only our Alwin was already back from the war. I don't even want to think that something might happen to him. I pray the Lord won't let it happen.

My dear Wilhelm, my health is not bad except for the old age pains and my eyes. They get worse every day. I cannot read a newspaper or letter any more. You don't know how hard it is for me to write a letter, so you are the only one I write to, everyone else Bertha is doing the writing. I am sure you can see it in my handwriting but I am happy I still can do it.

Enclosed my dear son you will find a picture of me and your brother and sister. We had it taken in Freiburg when we escorted Alwin to Dresden. From there he had to go to war. I wanted to have it enlarged but then we could not send it by mail. I also want to send one to my son-in-law but want to wait first if you receive this one.

Will close now (with) the wish that you will write us right away and then I will write you, to tell you how we are and especially Alwin.

Hope you are all well and with many hearty greetings,

> *Your sad father,*
> *August Kempe*

By summer 1871, August's vision has greatly deteriorated, Bertha writes to Wilhelm. August, 71, has visited a doctor in Dresden, which is about 35 miles away from their village of Sayda, and will soon have eye surgery. The fact that he was able financially to travel to Dresden and pay for eye surgery suggests that he was not a poor man.

Bertha also chides Wilhelm for not writing more frequently. She suggests that he return to Sayda, and that only such a major event could make her and their father happy again. Clearly, Bertha and August remain emotionally tied to Wilhelm, even 17 years after his departure, and seem to believe that much of their future happiness depends on him in one way or another.

In addition, Bertha writes that younger brother Alwin, the most likely person to take over the family farm in Wilhelm's absence, has returned home from the army, but he wants no part of a farmer's life. He would rather be a bartender in the city rather than a farmer in the country.

Dysfunction seems rampant in the family's internal relationships.

9. Bertha to Wilhelm – August 1, 1871, from Sayda

My Dearest Beloved Brother!

I do hope so much that this letter will reach you and your family doing fine. I wish I could say the same from us. Father is suffering terribly with his eyes, and every day his eyesight is getting weaker. He went to a famous doctor in Dresden who said that by September he had to have an operation. And even so Father is afraid of it, he decided to have the operation. And all we can do is pray that it will be a success.

Dear Brother, Father is so worried about you not writing us. We know you received our letter and photograph, since you wrote a small note with the letter from brother-in-law Mayer, but Father hoped for a long letter answering his questions. So please write us as soon as you can find time and give us your honest opinion about them.

I am so happy to tell you that Alwin came back from the war. With all the battles he helped in fighting he came back healthy and happy. It was a bad war; I am sure you read about it. We celebrated the peace here in Sayda with a beautiful concert and ball and danced the whole night through. Alwin will write you soon; he is already back in Dresden on the same job at the Hotel Bavaria, which he had before the war. His boss absolutely wanted him back and there was nothing we could do, even so that kind of life is not good for him. Father wants him to be here and take over the farm but he doesn't want it.

So often Father says, if only Wilhelm could come over here and take my property over, Him I could trust. I wonder if you couldn't sell your property and come back home. It would make us so very happy, but if you and your dear wife could not decide to come back home, then dear Brother could not you come for a visit so we could see each other and talk about so many things that should be straightened out. God would bless you and bring you safely home to your loved ones.

Bertha

Wilhelm's cousin Hermann Weigel writes to him for the first time in 1872. After a re-introduction, he provides more news of Wilhelm's father and brother and their rocky relationship.

Hermann's true reason for writing, it seems, is to seek Wilhelm's advice about joining him in America. The promise of a new life in a new land continued to beckon young Germans throughout the 19th century.

10. Hermann Weigel to Wilhelm – April 6, 1872, from Leipzig

My Dear Cousin Wilhelm!

Many greetings to you and your family. It is 18 years since we have seen each other and I wonder if you still can remember me. Since we have seen each other last, many things have changed. I worked for 11 years in the mill in [Mordengrund?]. I learned as a miller and baker but then I had to be soldier and was with the Cavalry for nine years and fought in both wars, 1866 in Austria and 1870-1871 in France. In 1866, I lost my only brother Edward, but I was lucky both times.

Now since September 1, 1871, I live here in Leipzig and work at the office in the Leipzig-Dresden Railroad. But being behind the desk all day is hard to take for me. Like you I was used since childhood to work hard in the fresh air and only feel well if I can work myself out, and that is the reason why I ask you for a favor and advice. For years I wished I had a way to come to America, but because I was a soldier it was not possible. And now I want to ask you if you think I could find work there. Please let me know as soon as possible what you think and if yes, which way is the best. I could quit my job right away.

My parents know about it and would not hold me back and so I am anxious to hear your opinion. Your brother Alwin also wrote me a few days ago. He is in Dresden as bartender, and he is very tired of that job but does not want to take over your father's farm, since he does not enjoy that kind of work from morning til night. And so he asked me to write you about him too. I would be happy to come together with him, since we both were always close as brothers and parting would be hard for us. But your father is not very happy about it and would like to keep Alwin here, so I have to go up to talk to him about it.

Now I will close my dear Wilhelm and hope to hear soon from you. With many hearty greetings from your brother Alwin, Father, and Bertha and from your

Cousin Hermann Weigel

Many hearty greetings to your family. I enclose my picture; it was taken while I was a soldier.

My address is:
Hermann Weigel
Main Office of the Leipzig-Dresden Railroad in Leipzig
Kingdom of Saxony

In a letter to Wilhelm seven months later, Hermann explains that he has not left Germany because his parents have become ill. He's disappointed. There's no evidence that Hermann ever came to the U.S. He hasn't been identified in U.S. immigration or census records.

This letter also indicates continuing discord in the Kempe family. Apparently, Wilhelm had asked Hermann to approach Wilhelm's father, August, for some items – unidentified in the letter – to be sent to Texas. August refused to turn them over, Hermann writes, and suggests that the Kempe family patriarch was less than cooperative on the matter. A subsequent note from August (see his November 29, 1872 letter) provides a different explanation, however.

Bertha and Alwin are doing well, Hermann writes, and his words add to evidence that Alwin is less than responsible and not faithfully meeting a son's expected obligations to his father.

Hermann is very concerned about the health of his parents, and in fact, his mother died a week after he wrote this letter. He also writes a line or two of the current circumstances of his sisters Christel and Marie, a shop owner.

11. Hermann Weigel to Wilhelm – November 12, 1872, from Leipzig

Dear Wilhelm!

I am sure you are waiting to get an answer from me, because it was my intention to visit you around September. My plans were changed because I was ill for quite some time and thought that I would not be able to come at all. But I am better now and thank God, I feel fine.

Now even my parents are since this summer very sick, especially my mother worries me. My father is also sick for a long time, but it is not dangerous. He has gout and [?] and often feels so bad that he can't walk. So for a short time he stands, then he sits down – this goes on day and night. I was several days visiting them, but it is so sad, when I see them suffer and can't help. Even the doctor tried several medications, but without results.

So you see that under these sad circumstances I am unable to leave them right now. I still hope that I come there and I plan to come next spring. Maybe the situation changes for the better. I already have prepared everything for my trip and have all what I need. I already mailed my certificate to Texas and I hope that I will have no further problems arise, not counting the sad illnesses of my parents.

A friend of mine left from Leipzig on September 1 and traveled again to New Orleans. He is already for quite some time there and I had planned on coming with him. Now he wrote to me that he reached New Orleans and so my yearning increased dramatically.

I told your father that you had written to me about what you need that I should bring along. He seemed to think that you don't need it and he was not going to pay for it. He still is like he was earlier. You know him. He is really lucky that the eye operation was successful and he can see again.

On other matters: Bertha and Alwin are doing fine, even your father. Alwin is still in Dresden [Translator's note: "Illegible word here, possibly referring to an occupation."] *and I am curious if he ever takes care of your father's business. I hope he finds an efficient wife. I am in the same situation, because I am not married either, and I don't have any prospects. On Sunday (Pentecost) I will travel to Dresden to visit my sisters and I plan on asking Alwin if he wrote to you lately because I told him several times, but you know he is often sulky.*

You know that my sister Christel and Peterlein are married in Dresden and I don't know if you know they have a little girl and they are happy. Marie also lives there and has a hat business.

Right now in Dresden they have a lot of activities going on, because our king celebrates his golden wedding anniversary and the German Emperor and Empress are here and also kings and counts from different countries.

The weather here is often bad; we have a lot of rain and had several storms. But nevertheless, we had a good crop this year in Germany.

Now I have to finish my letter and hope that you write back soon and I also hope that you and your family are healthy.

Many greetings to all of you.

Your cousin Hermann Weigel
Hotel Palmtree

In this lengthy letter, Wilhelm's father August, now 72, writes that after surgery and many weeks in a Dresden hospital, his eyesight is much better. He is weak, however. Before he dies, he wants to make sure that Bertha and Alwin will have the resources to live successfully on their own – although both are now well into their 20s.

August acknowledges, too, that Wilhelm has lost a child in Texas, a tragedy with which August can readily identify, having lost seven of his own, most as very young children. And August himself, with his sister Amalie, are the only two of nine siblings who reached adulthood. Their father, Karl Gottlieb Kempe, was the only one of three siblings to live past childhood.

August confirms more bad news. His sister "Mulune" [Amalie], mother of Wilhelm's cousin Hermann Weigel, has died. And Amalie's husband, August's brother-in-law, is in poor health. He also confirms Hermann's desire to come to America, and that his parents' illnesses have not allowed him to leave.

But August contradicts Hermann's November 12 letter, in which Hermann wrote that August was unwilling to send to Wilhelm items that he requested. Instead, August writes that since Hermann is no longer going to America, he has no way of sending the unnamed items to Wilhelm in Texas. August appears to have found a credible – if disingenuous – response to give Wilhelm and thereby not comply with his request. On the other hand, there's no indication of the precise nature of Wilhelm's request, so it might have been unreasonable, at least in the view of his aging father on the other side of the Atlantic.

August also complains to Wilhelm about Alwin's irresponsibility. August writes that he "would be patient" with Alwin in teaching him how to run the farm if Alwin would take it over. That statement alone suggests that August is not usually prone to showing patience with his younger son. Apparently as a last resort, August asks Wilhelm to write Alwin and encourage him to pursue a more constructive path in life.

12. August to Wilhelm [and Frederike] – November 29, 1872,
    from Sayda

My Dear Children!

Since I am doing a little bit better with my eyes, I am happy to write you again. I did not think that I could do it again, as my eyesight was almost gone, but through God's help I can read again through special glasses. But I have to be very careful with my eyes. It was a hard time for me when my eyes started to fail, and the doctors told me that the operation would be necessary. So I finally went to the hospital in Dresden where the first time I had to stay over nine weeks and the second time six weeks. But both operations were successful. The doctors told me that they themselves were surprised that my eyesight came back. It cost an awful lot of money, but I am willing to forget about that.

Today is already January 10, but I had to wait that long to finish this letter as the writing hurts my eyes and I have to apply a few times daily the medicine. But now I feel fine and I hope am able to finish this letter. I know you had to wait a long time for this letter, otherwise I am glad I am doing fine except that my legs won't carry me very far any more, but I hope I shall live a few more years until I know that Bertha and Alwin are taken care of.

My good Wilhelm, we were so happy when we received your letter on January 12 and were so sad to hear that you lost your dear child. I can feel the pain with you, you know how often this had happened to me, so that sometimes I thought I cannot take it any more and had to put my trust and hope in God.

I was very surprised to hear that you did not receive Hermann Weigel's letter. He told me he wrote you last August and we were sorry to hear that you had troubles because of it. Now I have to tell you very sad news. My good sister, Mulune Weigel, died on November 19. She had tuberculosis. She was very sick and in terrible pain. I had to stay on her bedside day and night and tried my best to comfort her. The bad thing is that my brother-in-law is so bad off too. He cannot walk any more nor sleep in his bed so he has to sit in his grandfather chair all the time because of his pains. So now I am staying with him every night until 12 o'clock to keep him company.

This dear Wilhelm was also the reason why Hermann could not come to you in America. He had to stay with his sick parents. His mother told him that if he would leave her now it would be her death, and so Hermann decided to stay here and keep his job in Leipzig. In October, he came here to Sayda to visit and he met Bertha's best friend. She is the daughter of Cantor Weigt, who passed on; she is a very good girl and also inherited 5,000 to 6,000 Thalers from her father.

My dear son, you asked for a few items, and believe me, I was not at all angry about it, but I don't know how to send it to you since Hermann did not come to you. But believe me, when the time comes to part my property you will be the first one to inherit.

I honestly don't know what to do about it; maybe you can give me some advice. Alwin makes me such trouble and gives me so much pain. I lost all my trust in him. If I could give him the farm I know it would be all lost since the Thaler is worth nothing in his eyes. He spends everything he gets. He made good money in his job but did not save a penny and had debts instead.

He now is in the age where a man should settle down, but he won't, he knows everything better. I talked with him so often about it and asked him to settle down and be like you, but I have no hope left. It worries me day and night.

Now you can understand why he does not even write. He could have done so as he had the time, but I should force him to do it. I know he would like best if I would give him a few hundred Thalers and tell him to go to America. Perhaps I would be better off, since I have no joy, just heartaches from him, but I don't want to let our property fall into strangers' hands.

But Alwin is just not interested in my farm, he does not care, does not want to work it, and if I would give it all to him and teach him and I would be patient with him it still would not help. Now dear Wilhelm, I wish you would write him and say your honest opinion. He might listen to you. I am sorry I have to trouble you with it but I need your help.

I also want to make my will in the near future. I kept on waiting with it since I did not know how it would be right but now I am afraid that I might not live too long any more.

It is possible that Bertha will get married this summer and she should not wait any longer, although it will be lonely for me then.

Our weather is beautiful here, no snow or frost, it is like summer with trees and flowers blooming. In a few weeks we might have strawberries. Last year was such beautiful weather too. Now, dear son, write me again soon and with many hearty greetings,

Your father,
August Friedrich Kempe

Wilhelm's brother Alwin continues to chafe at his father's expectations. In another rare and brief letter to his elder brother, Alwin tells of his wish to leave Sayda and perhaps join Wilhelm in Texas. He seeks Wilhelm's intervention in the ongoing battle of wills he has with his father.

13. Alwin to Wilhelm and Frederike – January 22, 1873, from Sayda

Dear Brother Wilhelm and Sister-in-Law,

I am so sorry I did not write you for so long but since I am back I worked very hard as a beer distributor [bartender?] in Dresden but after the first I do want to work in something different.

You said in your letter that you have so much land yet you cannot work. I wish I was with you to help you but Father does not want me to leave. You know I would like to take over the house and fields but I know I would be in debt over my ears and the girl I want to marry has 5 to 6 Thalers, and that doesn't help. The French war really messed me up again. If I had the money myself I still might come to you and start something.

My dear Wilhelm I sure wish you could come and see us again, it sure would help. I just cannot talk with Father and get along like you, that is the reason I am leaving this week again.

Thank goodness I am real healthy like a fish in the wa-
ter.
I do wish you would write me a letter once. I would be
very happy about it and will write you more often.
Many greetings to you and your family.

Your brother Alwin

Wilhelm's cousin Marie Weigel, sister of Hermann Weigel, sends what appears to be her first letter to Wilhelm in 1873. Wilhelm must have welcomed letters from his Weigel cousins. Their letters were generally happy in tone, in contrast to the self-absorbed notes he received from his father and brother, and to a lesser degree from his sister.

Marie notes, however, that her mother – August Kempe's sister Amalie – has died and that her father remains very ill. She further advises Wilhelm that his father August is not well, and that his vision problems have returned.

The Mrs. Lohse to whom she refers in the opening sentence of her letter remains unidentified. No letter from a Mrs. Lohse survives.

14. Maria Weigel to Wilhelm – September 5, 1873, from Sayda

My Dear Wilhelm!

Since Mrs. Lohse is sending you a letter, I am sending you a few lines along. I hope they will reach you in good health. From your last letter, we could see that you are doing all right, which made us very happy. I wonder if you can still remember me. We used to play a lot together as children and were so happy then but times have changed.

I think you know that my dear mother died in the last year in November and my father is very sick with arthritis and rheumatism and all the medicine will not help. I am glad I moved back here so I can take care of him as he can hardly sleep anymore.

My sister Christel is married two-and-a-half years now and has a little girl, one year old, which brings us much happiness. Hermann, Zienel, and Mienel are doing fine and we are all still single, but unless something good comes along, we had better stay that way.

Dear Wilhelm, I could write you so much more but since time is short I will have to hurry and tell you that your father is not doing too well. As you know he once had an operation on his eyes but it is now again as bad as it was before. I am sure Bertha has told you about it, but we just feel so sorry about him. Your father comes to visit us every evening and we sit and talk about all the good and bad things that happen to us. But if you believe in God, everything is much easier to take.

And now I will close with my best wishes and hardy greeting to your dear family.

Your cousin,
Maria Weigel

My father and my brother and sisters are sending you their best wishes, too. I put a little something in the letter for your little daughter. I am sorry it could not be more, but I hope it shows my love and good will.

Bertha's next letter brings news of more eye problems for August, but also word that another surgery in the city has succeeded in saving his vision.

She also mentions how good it feels to be able to take care of parents as they age, and writes that she knows Wilhelm would do the same if he had remained in Germany. Perhaps she means this sincerely and literally, but it's equally possible that she writes these words pointedly and sarcastically to Wilhelm, particularly after she struggled with their father's long hospitalization in Wilhelm's continued absence.

The battle of wills between August and Alwin continues unabated. Like her father, Bertha also wishes that Alwin would take over the farm, which she believes he could manage successfully. She implores Wilhelm to intercede by writing to Alwin and offering him good counsel.

Bertha saves her good news for last. After a long romance, she has become engaged to a postman surnamed Dietel. But even in marriage, she will have to take care of August, she notes.

15. Bertha to Wilhelm – January 15, 1875, from Sayda

My dear good brother!

I am very happy to answer your letter right away. We received your dear letter 9th of January. We just could not understand why we didn't hear from you for so long and father was ever so worried if he had hurt your feelings in any way. But now we fully understand why you could not write sooner and often things just don't go the way we planned it. That you are doing well and are healthy, we are very happy to hear.

Thank goodness we are doing all right only father's eyes are so bad and last summer he was again for two months in the hospital. Father is so strong even the doctors were surprised about his courage and ability to take pain. Over 10 days he had to lay in a dark room with bandaged eyes and was not allowed to move a muscle. He had a day and night nurse at his bedside and was not allowed to talk or eat. It cost a lot of money, but it saved his eyesight. We never go anyplace except to church on Sunday. It is a good feeling to be able to take care of your parents in their old age and I know if you were here you would do the same.

Father bought his cemetery lot a few years ago now he wants to have the bricks laid. He is always afraid he will die before his grave is fixed. I hope I will have him for many years to come and he is still full of will to live, but he says he keeps having dreams about having to die.

Alwin is in Gohlis near Leipzig as supervisor, but we are afraid he will not stay there too much longer. He just does not like to stay too long in one place. Also the people like him well. Father gets so angry at him for not writing to you. I wrote Alwin a letter and told him to please see life in a different way, to settle down and stop playing the big man but instead to save his money. He troubles father so very much but he will not change.

He could so easily go into the cattle business and that makes good money. A good horse costs 200 to 300 Thal-

ers, a cow 100 Thalers[24], a calf 15 to 18 Thalers and a pig 20 Thalers, also to buy a pound of meat is so expensive.

Last year we had here in the mountains a very good crop. Everything grew, even so, we had a very dry summer. You have too much water, it seems, and we have too little.

Dear brother, whenever you have the time please write to Alwin and tell him to please not worry father so. For my brother-in-law, Mayer, we did not hear from a long time. I wish he would have let us know that he moved. We are wondering how the children are doing and how their mother is treating them.

Many thanks for the greeting to Postman Dietel. He was so happy that you thought about him. He had two weeks vacation in July and we were engaged on the 15th of July. We made a trip with my father and his father during his vacation and had a wonderful time.

Dietel's father is getting a nurse from the city to take care of him and so he can put in for transfer to Sayda and if they will acknowledge that, we can get married. After all, I cannot leave father alone, so we have to settle down here in
Sayda and until now Dietel could not leave his father alone, either. You should see the beautiful letters he wrote to me during those years, since we were not able to see each other too often.

Bertha

After the death of his wife (and Wilhelm's sister) Auguste in late 1870, Wilhelm's brother-in-law John Mayer remarried in July 1871 and moved to the Bushdale community near Rockdale in Milam County.[25]

---

[24] The difficulty of determining a truly accurate value for the German Thaler in comparison to the U.S. dollar in 1875 should not be underestimated. Both were monetary units in distant lands with different economies that probably would have established different values for common commodities. It is interesting to note, however, that in Sayda the value of a cow was 100 Thaler in 1875. Also in 1875, Wilhelm was assessed $80 for 20 cows, or $4 each. Based on this simplistic data and analysis, $1 would have equaled 25 Thaler in 1875.

In this 1876 letter, he responds to a letter written to him by an unidentified nephew who was one of Wilhelm's sons. Wilhelm's eldest son, Wilhelm Jr., was 14 at the time. His next youngest brother, Herman, was 12. Either could have written a letter to Mayer.

Mayer notes that his daughter – a cousin to the nephew who wrote to him – is in school nearby after previous enrollment at a school in Colorado County (probably not far from the county line close to where John and Auguste Mayer lived in neighboring Austin County).

Also, the letter that Mayer says he sent to the nephew's parents (Wilhelm and his wife Emma) doesn't survive.

16. John Mayer to Wilhelm's son – March 17, 1876,
    from Rockdale

Dear Nephew Kempe!

Your letter dated March 5 we already received on the eighth of March. I was so happy to see that you did not forget your uncle Mayer and I am so happy to hear that you are studying so hard and I am sure that it will help you a lot later on.

Marie and [?] are going to school here. The school is only two miles away. We built it last fall but until now they only learned how to read and write English and some arithmetic. The two girls and one boy are the only two [Germans] in school. Marie I had in Colorado [County] in the school but last year on Christmas I brought her home.

Dear nephew, from your letter, I learned that your parents did not receive my letter yet. How come I do not know, since I wrote as soon as I had received theirs. It only could be possible that my son-in-law sent the letter

---

[25] Williams, Velmalene. Letter to Ray Grasshoff. On July 19, 1871 – less than a year after first wife Auguste's death in late 1870 – John Mayer married Katharina Gerngross in Colorado County. They soon moved to the Bushdale community near Rockdale in Milam County. With Katharina, Mayer fathered four more daughters in addition to the four he fathered with Auguste. Mayer died at 44 on December 5, 1876, when his wife was about two months pregnant with their last child.

off at a later date, since he also wanted to write a letter to them.

My wheat I already have in the ground but with the cotton I still wait since I am not sure about some more cold weather coming up.

Send greetings to your parents, also sister and brother and I hope to hear soon from you.

With love, your uncle John Mayer and family

Bertha's next letter brings another report of difficulty with Alwin, as well as news of her own more personal tragedy.

17. Bertha to Wilhelm and Frederike – November 15, 1876, from Sayda

Dearest brother and sister-in-law!

With all my heart I hope that my letter reaches you doing well and healthy. Thank goodness father is doing a little better. Even so, his eyes are still weak.

From our brother Alwin, we still know nothing. We could not find out where he lives, but Hermann Weigel promised to check with the military headquarters, since Alwin is still under obligation and therefore has to report his address to them.

So long we waited for your letter I hope you are not angry about something.

Dear brother, I am writing you today with a broken heart. I know you will feel with me my sorrow but I can hardly write it down. My loved fiancé Dietel died with a very sudden death. He made a trip to Dresden to visit his brother and when he arrived he felt very bad and complained about pains all over. Since he did not get better, he called the doctor. The doctor said it was rheumatic fever but not dangerous but after 10 days he had a brain stroke to it and it happened. He died on September 21. His brother sent a telegram to Sayda and the whole town got excited. Nobody had the heart to tell me. Everybody here honored and loved him.

I went then to his funeral, which was on the September 24, the same day our mother died. Father did not want me to go. He was afraid for me, but I had to see him because I still could not believe he was dead. It was terrible for me, believe me. I almost could not take it remembering that I knew him for 12 years, had loved him and only lived for him and our future and now I am alone and if I would not have father, I would not know what I would do. But because of him, I have to keep my head up.

Dear brother, I wrote you that Dietel worked at the post office here in Sayda since last year. The examinations for this job had been very hard and I wonder if studying for it did not bring his sickness on. And to think that this year we wanted to get married.

Now, dear brother, I have to tell you something else. It seems that in this letter I cannot write you something happy, just bad news. On June 8th, we had a terrible thunderstorm after a hot, dry heat wave, so down at the Friedebacher Way, the lightning struck a barn and spread and burned down 26 barns and there was nothing we could do about it. We received 500 Thaler for it but father said in his age and as things are with Alwin, he does not want to rebuild it.

I did not come any further with my letter and had to stop for a few weeks. But do not worry, father is still alive and doing well, but oh ...

Bertha

Another of Wilhelm's cousins from the Weigel family initiates contact with him in 1877. Clementine Weigel Einert, wife of Friedrich Einert, sends her greetings and an update on her life. Notably, she and her husband are raising the 17-year-old daughter of one of her sisters, but without further explanation. Possibly the sister has died.

Clementine also notes that Wilhelm's sister Bertha has married. The marriage is noteworthy since the engagement period was much shorter than the lengthy romance Bertha had with her first fiancé, who had died less than a year ago.

Also documented in this letter is Alwin's premature death, at about age 31. Clementine sends condolences, but there is little clue to the cause of his demise.

18. Clementine (Weigel) Einert to Wilhelm – November 29, 1877, from Sayda

My good Wilhelm!

In the hope that this letter will find you and your wife and children doing well. We are doing fine; only my husband is sickly for several years now. We have no family but a foster daughter, 17 years old. She is my sister's daughter. We have had her since she was two years old. She is a good help already. We have 40 scheffel[26] land, four cows, one calf, four pigs and Maria is very handy with them and a strong girl. We also have a blacksmith's shop and two helpers. Crops were good this year, so perhaps we will have a few hundred Thaler left over to put aside.

Well, dear Wilhelm, your sister Bertha is also married and lives in your father's house. I believe she has a good man. I hope he will have patience with her since she does not know anything about farming. They had a beautiful wedding. All my sisters and brothers were there, too, and wished you could have joined us.

When we talked about you and emptied our glass to your health, your father cried so hard. Since we hoped you would come and see us this summer, but we know that you cannot leave everything so fast behind and that we are so far apart. Bertha said that if you would come, she would gladly give you half of the farm. You both would have enough. I believe your father has a good hundred scheffel land. Bertha wants to buy some cows in the spring. Your

---

[26] "Scheffel" is an old German measurement of volume, not land area, so its appearance in this context, and later in this letter, must represent an error in translation.

father is so happy that Bertha was taken care of while he was still alive. We are so sorry that Alwin had to die such a terrible death last year. Nobody would have thought so. Your father had to go through so much pain already.

Now my dear Wilhelm, we have told you a lot of news and please write us soon again. Your sister Bertha always tells us about the news about you. My sisters Marie and Christel are married in Dresden, only my sister, Mienel, is still single. My brother Hermann married a very pretty wife. Now I want to greet all of you very heartily with many good wishes.

Your cousin,
Clementine Einert
Friedrich Einert
Maria Einert

We also wish you a Merry Christmas and a Happy New Year.

Wilhelm's cousin Hermann Weigel's next letter notes some discord in his family, too. He no longer is close to some of his sisters because of the religion they practice.

Hermann, now married to a woman named Emma, also details Bertha's wedding to another man named Dietel – the surname of her first fiancé as well. Although it's possible that she would be engaged in succession to two men with the same surname, or that she would marry a relative of her first fiancé, it's also possible that the translator erred in decoding either the first or second fiancé's name. But because the translator offered Dietel as the surname in all future letters from Bertha and her daughter, it must be the correct surname for Bertha's husband.

As do most other relatives and friends who write to Wilhelm, Hermann comments on Wilhelm's father. Hermann seconds the suggestion of others that Wilhelm return to Germany for a visit to discuss in person an unnamed issue with his father.

19. Hermann and Emma Weigel to Wilhelm – March 18, 1878, from Meissen

My Dear Wilhelm!

Since receiving your October 7 letter last year in early November, I thought daily about you and wanted to write you about important family matters but I had to spend long hours at work and was kept very busy.

I hope you hear the news about Bertha from your father. I wrote them that I had received your letter and how happy I was about it. The trust you showed me in your letter I do appreciate very much and I want to tell you that I always looked at you as a good and trusted friend. As you know my sisters and I have drifted apart and our love for each other has cooled. The reason is their change of religion. With exception of [your?] family they became members of a sect in Dresden of which I am deadly opposed. I was raised in my religion, believe in it and nothing can change that. Marie and Christel married members of this religion and since Mienel lives with them she also became a member of it. And so we never see each other even so we only live a few hours apart and otherwise have no reason to hate each other.

Shortly before I received your letter my wife and I went to Sayda to attend your sister's wedding. Bertha married the Agriculture Assistant Dietel from Dittmannsdorf. He is 28 or 29 years old and his family is a good and well-liked family. The wedding was in the church in Sayda. There were about 30 guests and after the ceremony we all rode in 10 carriages to Dittmannsdorf where the reception was held. We all thought of you and emptied a glass of wine as salute to you and your family, which we wined especially on this day. The wedding was a happy one and lasted until 6 o'clock in the morning. The young couple took an apartment on the first floor in your father's house since he wants to stay and work in Sayda. Bertha is not a strong woman and cannot work too hard and so the work on his father's big farm would be too much for her. Besides, she is also expecting a baby and we are very happy for the young people and do wish them the best for their future.

Your father is very happy about Bertha's marriage and that she is taken care of. He is doing all right for his high age but his eyes are getting very bad.

The letter you wrote to your father on April 20 of last year he has not received and I imagine the letter was lost. You wrote that you were afraid that your father would be angry about that letter. But I do not think so and advise you to write him once more about this matter as it is very good advice which he should know. But it is my opinion that the best thing would be your coming yourself and talking it over with him. I do trust Bertha and you know that, but a letter, which Bertha has to read to your father, can never accomplish what you yourself could do. Of course, this is only my opinion and I only write it to you as a friend.

Dienel is writing you also a few lines and you can see she still is only happy when she can work from morning til night.

I am happy to tell you that my wife and I are doing fine and that in about six months we are going to have a baby and I am so happy about it.

Now my dear Wilhelm I will close this letter. I do hope you did have a good crop this year and that the eye sickness which your family had last year is over with and left no damage to either one of you. I hope that once in a while you can buy a German newspaper and so will know what is happening over here.

> *With many friendly greetings to you and your family!*
> *Yours, Hermann and Emma Weigel*

Please write soon again. My address is still:
Station [Office Clerk?] *in Meissen*

Chapter Five

LETTERS:
1879 AND WILHELM'S VISIT
TO GERMANY

In 1879, Wilhelm responds to the wishes of his friends and family in Germany and returns for a visit of several months. He's been away from his homeland for 25 years.

Over the course of several letters to his wife Frederike, who has remained in Texas, he tells of visiting relatives and friends he had not seen in decades.

Initially, he writes of the beauty of the German landscape and the joy of returning, but later develops a less favorable impression of the lifestyle there.

The letter's greeting to the Kaase family in Texas probably refers to Frederick and Henriette Kaase and their family. Henriette is Frederike's sister.

20. Wilhelm to Frederike – May 28, 1879, from Meissen

Dearest Wife!

To your happiness and satisfaction I want to write you that our Lord brought me safely to my beloved German Fatherland. On May 4, I left New Orleans with the ship Nuernburg as I had written you before. And on May 27 I arrived in Bremen.

The trip was pretty good; we had strong winds but no real storms. Many of the passengers were very seasick but it did not bother me too much.

There were about 130 passengers aboard. But my thoughts were always with you at home. So I was rather unhappy since I could not find anyone to have a good honest talk with. There were all kinds of people aboard, French, English, Italians, also from Ireland, Sweden, Austria and from many parts of Germany. Some also came *from Texas but I did not like one of them. The only nice one was from New Orleans, a saddle maker, who also went for a visit to Germany. He had $800 with him, and since one man had his money stolen, I did not even dare to sleep well at night.*

Now my dearest Frederike I do pray that you and all our children are well and that I soon will be back with all of you.

Yesterday morning at 8 o'clock, May 28, I left Bremen by train via Uelsen, Stendal, Magdeburg, [Leethen?], Halle, Leipzig to Meissen where I arrived at midnight. Someone brought me to Hermann Weigel's home, where I had to awaken them since they had expected me four days earlier. Because he cannot leave his office alone, I will go on alone to Sayda by tomorrow, but he will join me later.

Dear wife you cannot imagine the luxury and fine living here, everybody seems to be rich.

Please write me right away and do hire some people to work for you and let me know if all is well. Do not worry as I will take care of everything when I am back. Also tell me how your father's doing and let the children write a few lines and address the letter to Sayda like I wrote it down for you.

On sea it was very cold and I did miss my overcoat badly. Germany has a very late spring this year. On the train I thoroughly enjoyed the beautiful view but the train goes so fast that everything passes much too fast.

Everybody complains about bad times but everybody lives in luxury and believes that the people in America have money to throw away.

Dearest wife, that is all the news I have but I will write you again as soon as I have seen my father. Please say hello to your father, and the Kaase family, and Schulenburg and to old Brueger. The Lord bless you all.

Your loving husband, W. Kempe

21. Wilhelm to Frederike – June 4, 1879, from Sayda

Dearest Wife!

Hope you received my letter from Meissen where I told you that I arrived well in Germany. I stayed with Hermann for two days. On Saturday, I left to Dresden, Freiburg, and to Bienenmuehle, where to my surprise my father and my brother-in-law waited for me. Bienen-muehle is two hours from Sayda.

Father is still doing all right and even so his eyesight is failing him he still can get around. I was worried I would find a sick man but I am so happy that this is not the case.

Dear wife I must tell you that when I saw my beloved Germany I cried. There is only one Germany with its beautiful country and buildings. But the people changed. Everywhere you go they seem to live just to enjoy life and its luxuries. But don't worry my dear Frederike, even so we do live much quieter and simpler and have to do without many things, we are just as happy and satisfied.

There are few people left in Sayda that I know and many have died.

I also saw Bertha and her little daughter, also her husband and stepdaughter. They are all doing well and were very happy to see me.

Please write me soon and let me know that you are doing all right and that nothing bad has happened. Even so it is wonderful to be here. I am always worried about you and my family since I am so far away from you.

Dear wife, don't worry about me, don't work too hard, and hire people to work. I will take care of everything when I am back.

When I leave Germany, I have to come back via New York. I am afraid it will cost a lot more and so I want to know what you think about it.

Let me know how your father is doing and say hello to the Kaase family and Schulenburg and Brueger. Please take care of yourself.

Your loving husband, Wilhelm Kempe

In his next letter, Wilhelm's reference to "the release in La Grange" and a cryptic reference to "my Galveston newspaper" remain unexplained. La Grange is the county seat of Fayette County, and Galveston is a coastal city in Texas.

Frederike will soon have another burden to suffer in Wilhelm's absence. Her father, Gottlieb Laas, died at 71 on June 30, 1879.

22. Wilhelm to Frederike – June 15, 1879, from Sayda

Dearest Wife,

Your letter of June 10 I received and was glad to hear that you and the children are healthy and doing well. I was so happy to hear that.

I am doing well and this is the third letter I am writing to you and hope you will receive them all.

I am glad to hear that the fields are all finished, now when nothing else bad happened, things will be all right. Don't worry about the release in La Grange, that is in order and also my Galveston newspaper, nobody is interested in that any way.

I must say I don't like it here any more. Everything here is so fine and proper and grand and when I am invited to go out I wonder if I am dressed right. The same thing happened when I visited Lauterbach's parents in Bremen, everything is much too fine for me.

Dear wife, I would love to bring you a few presents home but when I go home via New York it will cost so much more money.

Please write once more after this letter. Even if I am already gone it will make the family here happy to read your letter. Also let the children write a few lines.

With God's help I will see you all soon and well.

Your loving husband, Wilhelm

Many greetings from the family also to your father and all of our friends.

In this short letter from Hermann Weigel to Wilhelm while Wilhelm is visiting Germany, Hermann provides addresses for two of his sisters. Possibly Wilhelm plans to visit them.

23. Hermann Weigel to Wilhelm – July 7, 1879, from Köln an der Elbe

Dear Wilhelm,

According to your wishes I am sending you the addresses. They are B. Rossberg, Dresden, Polierstrasse No. 9 and Peterlein (Peter) [anban?] Schoenfeld near Leipzig, Marktplatz No. 4, third floor.

I hope you have also received the letter which I enclosed with Einert's, in that I expect that you are very well. I ask you to give hearty greetings to your family. I hope we will soon see each other again. You'll let me know when you come so that we can see you again.

With greetings,
Your Hermann

This note, apparently from a travel agent, indicates Wilhelm's plans for returning to America. His visit to Germany lasted approximately three months.

Note the reference to other passengers that are apparently associated with Wilhelm. Emigration records from Bremen were destroyed by German authorities long ago, or otherwise lost in World War II. But the passenger list provided upon the Mosel's arrival at New York on August 30, 1879 survives.[27] The list, dated September 1, 1879, includes the name Wilhelm Kempe, but no other names recognizable as people who might be associated with him. The visual quality of the list is poor, however, making names difficult to recognize.

---

[27] Ancestry.com. *New York Passenger Lists, 1820-1957* [database on-line]. Provo, UT, USA: The Generations Network, Inc., 2006. Original data: Passenger Lists of Vessels Arriving at New York, New York, 1820-1897; (National Archives Microfilm Publication M237, 675 rolls); Records of the U.S. Customs Service, Record Group 36; National Archives, Washington, D.C.

24. Carl Ludwig Bödeker to Wilhelm – August 7, 1879, from Bremen

Mr. Wilhelm Kempe
Sayda near Freiburg, Saxony

Received your letter dated 5th of this month and re-
served your room on the Mosel leaving on the 15th of this
month. Expect you here on said date.
If possible, you can send me the passage money for the
other passengers now, but the people can also pay it when
you arrive.

With friendly greetings,
Carl Ludwig Bödeker

Chapter Six

LETTERS:
THE 1880s

Wilhelm's 1879 visit to Germany raised interest in emigration among his acquaintances there. One of them was August Ferdinand Einhorn, who writes to Wilhelm in Texas with questions about joining him to escape high prices and taxes.

25. August Ferdinand Einhorn to Wilhelm – November 14, 1879, from Neu-Weigsdorf

Dear Mr. Kempe,

I went to see my brother-in-law in Sayda who made the boxes and the cabinet for you[28] and he told me that you had been here on visit last summer. So I went to see your father and he told me many interesting things about America. As you know, by next year I would like to go to America and I would like very much to settle down in the same town where you are, so I have a German friend close by that could help me with advice when necessary and your father said that he was sure that you would be happy to have good people around.

I am a linen weaver by profession, have a house here and leased some field to work, and I am wondering what to take along to America, and what is hard to get, since I have many good farm tools and equipment.

---

[28] According to family legend, a large wooden trunk now possessed by the author was brought from Germany by Wilhelm Kempe. Possibly it is ones of the "boxes" or the "cabinet" referenced in this letter. For many years, Wilhelm's grandson, Herman Grasshoff, stored feed for cattle in the trunk. Herman's daughter-in-law, Martha Powers Grasshoff, obtained it from him, had several coats of paint removed, and otherwise restored it to its original condition.

I have three sons, 18 years, 16 years, and 9 years old, and one girl 6 years old.

I imagine the trip would cost several hundred Thalers, and I wonder where my family and I would stay.

Here in Germany everything gets more expensive. I have to pay 26 Thaler tax a year.

I was so sorry to hear about your sick wife. My brother-in-law and sister told me to send greetings.

I hope that this letter will reach you in good health and that you would send me an answer soon.

My address is:
August Ferdinand Einhorn
Neu-Weigsdorf by Ainewalde
Saxony, Oberlausitz

Here you see I was telling the truth. [Translator's note: "Bill for advertisement in newspaper – House-sale 1.40"]

Bertha's next letter to Wilhelm expresses happiness that Frederike, Wilhelm's wife, has recovered from an illness.

She also notes August Ferdinand Einhorn's interest in emigrating to America She praises the man's qualities and asks Wilhelm to help him make the move.

Even though married with children, Bertha continues to take care of father August. She and her family live with him in the Kempe homestead. She writes that August's health and mood are declining rapidly.

26. Bertha [and others in name] to Wilhelm – January 5, 1880, from Sayda

My Dear Brother!

I do hope with all my heart that this letter will find you doing well. We are worried whether your wife is well again and we are so sorry that she has been so sick while you were away. And we hope that your presence will help her to get well fast.

We were so happy when we heard that you arrived well in America. Especially since you were always so sad and worried over here about your family, we prayed that you would make it back to your family in good health and are so glad that you arrived safely.

We also were sorry to hear that you had so much trouble with your baggage and that is was so expensive. But you must remember America is a long way from here.

I do hope that your wife and children are happy about the beautiful things you brought them and did Emma fit the dress and jacket? Did you also see Gustel's [Auguste's] children? What did they have to say?

Dear Brother, did you receive a letter from a man named August Ferdinand Einhorn from Neu-Weigsdorf near Cunewalde? He wants to emigrate to America and his brother-in-law, Kolbe, the cabinet maker, advised him to write to you. He is a very good man. He was born in [Albernau?]. He visited us a few times and also his wife and children would love to go to America. He figures he would need about 400 Thaler traveling money. What do you think about that?

Dear Brother! Father is not doing so well lately. He has to stay in bed and has a very hard time breathing, and his cough gives him such pain that sometimes he just screams. So we put his bed downstairs in the living room, that way I can stay with him during the night. If he only would be in a better mood. But he is afraid that he has to die and so he just is in a terrible mood as you saw when you were here.

The weather is terrible and so was the crop, most of it ruined by rain and cold weather. Even the cabbage and potatoes are bad. We have cold and snow here now, you cannot imagine. The only thing is to stay close to the stove. How was your crop and did your cotton turn out all right?

That is about all I know for today. Please write us as soon as possible, especially how your wife is doing, and let us know what you think about the Einhorn family. They will come to visit us soon again and then I will know what to tell them.

All your friends are sending their best wishes. They ask me so often how you are doing and whether you wrote. They really do like you a lot, even so you are not as good looking and handsome as you think you are.

With my best wishes and that the new year will bring you lots of happiness.

Your Father, Sister, and Brother-in-Law

Please write [?emmerick] a letter; he would be very happy about it.

[August] Ferdinand Einhorn remains keenly interested in coming to Texas to escape a poor economy in Germany, he says. His practical questions about life in Texas and how he and his family can cope offer insight into European knowledge of Texas. The first German immigrants to Texas in the 1830s and 1840s must have had similar questions, but mostly had no one to ask for accurate information before they crossed the Atlantic. They came anyway, forced to use their wits to adjust to life in the Texas frontier – and making their decisions to leave their homeland even more remarkable.

27. [August] Ferdinand Einhorn to Wilhelm – April 4, 1880, from Neu-Weigsdorf

Dear Friend Kempe,

You dear letter I received on April 3. I was in the field working so the mailman came especially out to give it to me the letter was very welcome. You are a dear friend to us and I hope we will see each other soon.

As you know this is my second marriage. In my first marriage I had five children and only one, my eldest son, is still alive. So you know how much sorrow I went through.

I think I have to sell my property cheap as times are bad and by the time I paid for the moving I am happy I will

have 600 Thalers left plus the tickets for me and my family which costs about 400 Thalers. I will reach you with about 200 Thalers in my pocket. But the way you write me, that we can find work and start anew we are willing to take the risk. And since I am not able to buy property over there, I will have to rent.

You wrote you wanted to build a second house. Why don't you wait until we are with you? I am bringing all my tools and will so be able to help you a lot. My sister's second son wanted to come with me but he is now home and sick and her eldest son is married.

What I would like to know is, do you have clay to make bricks? And my wife would like to know, what you use for washing clothes, shall she bring her tubs along, also how do you make butter and store it, since we heard you have no cellars? And how about the bedding, over here it is cold and there is lots of snow. Do you think we will need nets against insects at night? I had a bad cold now and hope it soon will be better.

The orders you sent me I will try to fill right away. I am sending many greetings to your dear family and hope that my letter reaches you in the best of health.

Sincerely yours,
Ferdinand Einhorn

The coats I will buy in Sayda and the materials I also will pick myself.

Bertha continues to be impressed with August Ferdinand Einhorn. Writing to Wilhelm at the end of 1880, she touts Einhorn as a quality person to join him in Texas.

As is typical, her letter includes bad news too. Father August's health continues its decline, farming in Sayda continues to face the vagaries of weather, cousin Christel Weigel Peterlein has died, and Bertha's husband's sister-in-law has died.

28. Bertha to Wilhelm – December 20, 1880, from Sayda

Dear Brother!

I hope that all of you received my letter and are doing well. We are fine except father. This winter his arthritis is bad again, especially his legs and feet are badly swollen.

I know you waited for a letter a long time but we were very busy with the farming. And the weather is so unstable with rain and hail so we finished harvesting very late. Our wheat crop was fairly good but we almost had no oats and even half of the potatoes were bad. And to top it all, one of our cows got sick and we had to sell it, so we had quite a loss this year.

Dear brother, I hope you also received the letter that Mr. Einhorn from Neu-Weigsdorf wrote you. The poor man was so embarrassed and sad that he could not go with you last fall. My man visited him a few days ago; we wanted to know what kind of people they are, so we could tell you. August [Bertha's husband] went to the cattle market to buy two cows, which was near Neu-Weigsdorf and stayed overnight with the family Einhorn. They treated him very nice and Mr. Einhorn even walked with him for six hours to the cattle market and was very helpful with the buying. August likes the people very much, they seem to be very busy and clean people and will do well in America. The man does everything himself, also built himself a good wagon and a lot of other things. We believe you won't go wrong with them. But he has to sell his property here first and it is a bad time for selling now and also the laws and taxes are terrible here. So he probably will come to America by next year. He is selling linen on the side to save money and meet the bills. If he should get a letter from you, he would be a very happy man.

Dear brother, I suppose you heard that Christel Peterlein, you met her last year, died suddenly. I feel so sorry for the four children. Also, the wife of August's oldest brother died, only 36 years old. She lived in Gruenburg.

Bertha

In another letter to Wilhelm, [August] Ferdinand Einhorn tells of his continuing efforts to plan for a move to Texas – part of an exodus that has already taken a considerable number of local families. Many of his generation continue to leave their homeland.

Einhorn reports that the people are leaving because of poor conditions in Germany. The nature of these conditions isn't clear, but seems to be related to the economy. This notion contradicts Wilhelm's comments from only two years earlier, when he visited the country and noted the people lived in luxury.

Perhaps the discrepancy is rooted in the relative experiences of each observer. Wilhelm had lived in rural Texas for many decades without much of anything that could be considered a luxury. He had become comfortable and satisfied with that kind of life, and observed wasteful extravagance – in his view – when he visited Germany in 1879. In contrast, the standard of living for many of his contemporaries in Germany probably continued at a relatively higher level compared to that in Texas. When that standard took a fall, no matter how slight, younger people were bound to look for alternatives to their view of a country in decline. In short, as Wilhelm and his German friends looked at the same conditions, Wilhelm saw the glass as half full, with quality of life having come a long way. But Germans saw it as half empty, with quality of life not near where it should be.

29. August Ferdinand Einhorn to Wilhelm – March 9, 1881, from Neu-Weigsdorf

Dear Friend Kempe!

I received your letter on February 28, and was so happy to receive it as I was waiting it anxiously. When I received your letter and read it I was very sad as I went through the same thing, as my first wife had the same sickness. But I want you not to despair as my wife recovered from it and became well again and so your dear wife will be well again. Only many years later did she get a liver ailment and after terrible pains had to die. I just could not believe it possible that she was gone, and only my prayers to God helped me get over it. It is terrible to have sickness in your family.

Believe me, I forever am thankful to you for bringing us to America. I know you will help me and my family to get a start. If I only had my property sold already, so we could be together and share our sorrows and problems. Times are bad here and so many people are going to America, 16 families here alone. The houses are getting cheaper every day, and are not selling at all.

My present wife is very happy about the idea to go to America and she is strong and healthy and a hard worker and so are the children.

We pray every day that someone will come and buy our property, but buyers are rare and I cannot give it away as we need the money to come over to you. Thank goodness the crop was a good one.

Will now close my letter and pray that the Lord will bless you and make your wife well again.

August Ferdinand Einhorn and family

Wilhelm's father August died in April 1884. Bertha's letter that apparently gave Wilhelm the news is missing from this collection.

A subsequent letter from Bertha, written a few months later, suggests that August left some of his estate to the children of his late daughter, Auguste, in Texas. The four girls, who now range in age from 16 to 26, had moved with their father John Mayer from Austin County to Milam County in 1873, following their mother's death in 1870. John Mayer died at age 44 in December 1876, when the oldest daughter was only 18.

Wilhelm was involved in helping the girls – his nieces – get their inheritances from their grandfather, several letters indicate.

30. Bertha to Wilhelm – June 28, 1884, from Sayda

My Dear Brother!

I am waiting daily to get a letter from you.
I am sure you received the letter with the sad news about Father and in which I asked you to give me the papers

about Gustel's [Auguste's] children, which I will have to bring to the courthouse. Especially their names and ages. I told them you would write it and they just had to wait for it.

Father's property also has been taxed and is in a court now, I wish there would not be so much excitement and paper work after someone dies but that is the way it is and mostly I am worried about the children. And, of course, it also is in your interest.

I do hope I will receive your letter soon. Your last letter we received and were happy about it.

Will close now and perhaps the court will write you too. With many greetings.

Your loving sister,
Bertha

I do miss Father so terrible.

31. Unidentified to Wilhelm – February 16, 1885

Honored Kempe!

Sending you power of attorney for B. Langer and rest of papers. I expect that you will have your signature verified by a notary public and then send the papers registered. My opinion is you would do well to put your share in 60-day draft in to New York, Galveston, or New Orleans payable in gold. You buy a 60-day draft cheaper than the other kind.

The "B. Lowenstein" who wrote a late-1885 letter to Wilhelm regarding legal matters was probably Benjamin Lowenstein of Rockdale, Milam County, Texas. From late 1873 until 1895, Lowenstein operated a successful mercantile business in that city. He also served as president and a member of the board of directors for the First National Bank of Rockdale, and was a member of the local school board as well. The nieces lived in the area, and the letter seems to refer to legal issues related to their inheritance from their late grandfather, August Kempe, in Sayda.

32. B. Lowenstein to Wilhelm – December 21, 1885, from Rockdale

Mr. Wilhelm Kempe
Flatonia

Dear Friend,

Received your favor from the 8th of this month with enclosure and today according to your request, after receiving power of attorney from the German Consul, I sent it to Mr. Robert Langer, Sayda, in Sachsen and hope that with this the matter is settled.
You I wish the best of health and a long life, greeting you and your family cordially.

Your friend,
B. Lowenstein

Part IV

A New Generation

Chapter Seven

LETTERS:
THE LATE 1890s AND EARLY 1900s

A new generation of German relatives begins to write to Wilhelm in the late 19th century. They include Marcus Rudolph, who writes to introduce himself as the fiancé of Wilhelm's niece, Marie Dietel, who is Bertha's daughter.

33. Marcus Rudolph to Wilhelm – April 17, 1898, from Sayda

Honorable Mr. Kempe!

> *Often we the family Dietel and I, especially my future bride, your niece, talk about you. And every time I wish I could meet you, especially since you are the only uncle on Marie's mother's side. Of course, as circumstances are, I know you are not able to come here. So I am taking the opportunity to write and send you my photograph.*
>
> *As your sister, my mother-in-law, wrote you, I am a businessman and have a department store here. We will be married in a few weeks and we only wish that besides my bride's parents, your nephew Karl, my sister, two brothers and wives, you Dear Uncle, could be here and celebrate with us.*
>
> *I do hope very much to hear soon from you.*
> *With many greetings.*

> *Yours,*
> *Marcus Rudolph*

In a separate letter, niece Marie Dietel also sends her greetings, and congratulates Wilhelm's son Bernhard on his marriage. Bernhard, known later to his descendants as Ben, married Maggie McGill in early 1898.

Marie refers also to "Aunt Rossberg" and explains in a parenthetical note that she is the former Marie Weigel. But Marie Weigel is a cousin to Wilhelm and Bertha, and therefore she is not a biological aunt to Bertha's daughter.

Marie also notes that "Aunt Rossberg" has "three grown daughters," and includes a 16-year-old in that group, offering an interesting view of when childhood is considered to be completed.

34. Marie Dietel to Wilhelm – April 19, 1898, from Sayda

My Dear Uncle!

I would like to enclose a note with my mother's letter and tell you many thanks for the letter you sent me, and do hope that our letters will reach you doing fine. I also hope that all my cousins are fine and wish that I could meet them personally. We are so happy about Bernhard's marriage and are sending our best wishes to the newlyweds

Yes, dear uncle, I also will take the serious step and will marry on May 31, at one o'clock, and do hope that you will think of me. I wish you could be here. My future husband is very interested in your family and so we talk a lot about you.

Many greetings from Uncle and Aunt Rossberg and their children. (Aunt Rossberg is the former Marie Weigel.) I went to visit them this week in Dresden. They have five children, three grown daughters aged 21, 19, and 16, a boy 14, and a little girl 10. He is a preacher here in Dresden.

With many greetings to you and your family.

Your Niece,
Marie Dietel

After her wedding, Marie thanks Wilhelm for his gift.

35. Marie Dietel Rudolph to Wilhelm – August 12, 1898, from Sayda

Dearest Uncle!

Please excuse my not writing you sooner but today I take the opportunity to write a few lines with Mother's letter. First of all I would like to thank you so very much for your wedding present. We were so very surprised and happy about it.

We do wish so very much that you could be closer to us, and that we could see and talk with you.

I am sure Mother wrote you all about the wedding so I don't have to do so.

My husband is such a very good man and treats me so well. I am trying very hard to learn all about his business and there is a lot that has to be learned about it.

Will close for now and hope that you and your family are doing fine.

With all my best wishes.

Your niece,
Marie,
and husband

In 1903, Bertha is 59, suffers from an unnamed health issue and will undergo surgery soon. Her son Karl also suffers from an unnamed but serious ailment. Beyond those troubles, Bertha provides updates on other friends and family.

36. Bertha to Wilhelm – February 3, 1903, from Sayda

Dear Brother,

I have received two letters from you and haven't answered them yet but I will do that now. You must forgive me. My illness is partially to blame, and then I have to spend so much time in bed because of the care for Karl where I can do only the most necessary things. He isn't well at all. It's very difficult for him to breathe. When he eats something it usually comes back up. He can't keep so much on his stomach anymore. His body is thin although we give him the most nourishing warm foods. Nothing helps, however, and one feels so sorry about it. It breaks one's heart to see the poor innocent person suffer so.

It is also destroying me. I must also succumb when one has to bear such sorrow and worry and all kinds of cares for so many years. I can't get away from my troubles so easily. I feel everything so deeply although I try to endure everything in patience trusting in God. However, one is and remains a human, a weak being, which can be torn apart. It has had such an effect on my body so that I have become sick.

Something is wrong with me all over. I just drag around and can't step out firmly any more. I am never a minute without pain. I'm going to have an operation which will be very difficult for me. I would never have thought that so many hardships would be placed upon me. Now, I only feel sorry for my children if I should not survive. They still need me so much. Now I'll wait and see for a few weeks yet then the season of the year is so bad. Then I would have to go to Dresden to the gynecology clinic where it costs five Marks a day. I would have to stay at least four to five weeks and this would amount to a nice sum of money which we naturally had not counted on. But nothing helps and one must put up with the most difficult things.

Now, dear brother, how are you? I hope you are well which I wish from the bottom of my heart. May God give you health and a peaceful life until the end of your life.

Your friend, Robert Langer, is also well. He is fat and has a very red face from drinking a lot of wine. Two of his daughters want to marry now and he is complaining very much that it costs him so much then he lost 30 to 40 thousand in the Leipzig bank that went bankrupt but no one feels sorry for him.

[Mienel?] is not now in Sayda, but in Rauschenbach, two hours from here with the farmer Mienel Einert, who has a large saw mill and is very rich. There [Mienel?] has a nice place and is well. They don't want to let her go but Hunhalts here wants to have her also. They are expecting her soon. Good old [Mienel?] is everywhere in demand. She received your short letter and will write you again before long.

I'm supposed to send you cordial greetings from our Marie and her husband. They visited us a few days ago. They'll also write you before long. Just think, dear brother, your kind dear letter in October was received on the 23rd, just the day of our silver wedding anniversary. Our joy was doubled as we received so many letters of good wishes from all families. Our children, grandchildren, and relatives came and showered us with presents.

Also, many cordial greetings from our Karl. If he felt better he would write you a long letter. Dear brother, have you received the picture postcards of Sayda?

Sincere greetings from
Your sister and brother-in-law

Please write soon.

Later in 1903, Wilhelm's niece and Bertha's daughter Marie writes with news that Bertha's surgery was a success. Marie also tells Wilhelm of her happy life and family, but is concerned about the health of her brother Karl.

37. Marie Dietel Rudolph to Wilhelm – (April?) 4, 1903, from Deutsch-Neudorf

God Greet You!
Dearest Uncle!

For weeks I wanted to write you and I do hope that this letter will find you doing well.

*Your last letter to our mother I had to bring to the hospi-
tal and she was so happy to receive it. The poor soul went
through so much pain but was so patient and trusted in
God. On February 26, father brought her to the city hospital in Dresden and on March 2 they operated on her from
10:15 in the morning until 10:45. Thank goodness everything went alright. They had to remove a tumor and some
liquid and three weeks later they had to take another
seven liters of liquid. And that made her very weak. She
could not sleep and had troubles with her stomach. But
now she is doing much better.*

*My husband bought a lumber factory here on April 1.
We paid 37,000 Marks for it. There is a beautiful house
behind it on top of the hill where we now live. The factory
has steam machinery with 60 horsepower and it also de-
livers the electricity for the town here. But we had to make
several repairs first and buy new things and it did cost a
lot of money. In two weeks the factory will open and we do
hope very much that we did the right thing.*

*We have two children, a girl four years old and a boy
two years old. They are good and healthy children. I am
so glad they inherited my husband's healthy nature*

*My brother Karl has to go through so much pain also
and as he now is older and understands he sometimes is
so without hope and wonders what the future will bring
him. If only he will not be bedridden for so long whenever
it comes to the worst, that worries my parents, especially
mother, so much. But we have to trust the Lord that he
knows the best.*
[Continued?]

Marie Dietel Rudolph

Only two months later, Bertha's health has again deteriorated as
Marie writes in her next surviving letter to Wilhelm. Karl is suffering
as well.

The brevity of a letter with such dire news is curious, but perhaps
understandable if Wilhelm has not responded – as suggested by Marie –
to a previous letter that probably provided more detail.

38. Marie Dietel Rudolph to Wilhelm – June 19, 1903, from Sayda

Dearest Uncle,

For quite a while now I am here with my parents, since my mother is still so very sick and I just did not get around to write you.

Mother is waiting so to hear from you and is afraid something happened to you since I received no answer from you for my last letter, two months ago, which I sent from my home in Deutsch-Neudorf, and in which I told you about Mother's sickness. I do hope you received the letter.

Since the operation Mother is doing so bad and is very seriously ill, also my brother Karl is not doing well at all. Thank goodness Father is still in good health.

I would be so happy if we could hear from you soon, and with many greetings from afar.

> *Your niece,*
> *Marie Dietel Ruldoph,*
> *with parents and brother*

Marie's letter to Wilhelm to tell him of Bertha's death at 59 on August 11, 1903 is missing from this collection. But another letter from Marie soon follows and brings word that Marie's sickly brother Karl has also died.

39. Marie Dietel Rudolph to Wilhelm – September 15, 1903, from Deutsch-Neudorf

Honorable Dear Uncle!

You surely are surprised to hear from me so soon again after I just wrote you a letter telling you about my mother's passing on. But the same sad thing I have to tell you again, and this time it is my brother Karl who died just two weeks after mother's death. On the 27th of August at 10:45 p.m. he followed my mother into eternity. It was very sudden. He came with Father the Sunday before to see us and then on Monday we all drove to Sayda to have Mother's will read. The following Sunday Karl wanted to move in with us so I could take care of him with Mother gone, but then Thursday it just happened. He hemorrhaged three times within half an hour and just died. The funeral was on August 31. He, like mother, had many flowers. He is directly beside mother.

Karl, like me, would have missed mother terribly. Father is quite different and seems to get along without any one and is not at all as sensitive as Mother and Karl were.

My husband is such a good man and Mother always got along so well with him. I am feeling terrible inside and do have to watch out that I am not making life hard for my dear ones.

Mother had stated in her will that Father should get one-fourth of her property and we children the rest. And of course from Karl, Father will now get one-third and we the rest. Father may not like it well but I do want to live in peace with him.

We will now close and hope you will write me soon as you are my relatives from my mother's side.

With many hearty greetings to you and your four children,

Your niece,
Marie Rudolph born Dietel

EPILOGUE

Wilhelm F. Kempe lived a long and eventful life – a life about which little would be known or remembered without the letters that he and his descendants kept for decades, and now for more than a century. So he lives on, while many others before and after him do not. Unfortunately, in today's age of brief and ephemeral electronic communication, few people write letters of any kind, much less with pen and ink, making less certain the availability of personal letters to shine light on people's thoughts and beliefs. The trend points to a disturbing loss of personal insight and legacy for future generations.

Wilhelm's remarkable life took him from the small European farming village of Sayda to travels as a young man throughout German provinces, across the Atlantic to the near-frontier of rural Texas, to the American Midwest as the country warred with itself, back to farming at his adopted home in Texas, on a return to Germany for a final visit with friends and aging relatives, back again to his New World family and friends in Texas, and then quiet, more peaceful senior years, the last spent living with a son and his family in Central and later South Texas.

The letters document that life and offer intriguing insights into the bigger picture challenges that confronted 19th century immigrants as well as their family members who remained in Europe. Emigration's effect on them has seldom been so documented.

Most obviously, the letters illustrate the deep loss and frustration felt by family in Germany after Wilhelm comes to Texas. Decades after his departure, and with no apparent hint to them that he has any desire to return, his father and younger siblings still cling to hope that he will leave America for the life that had been expected of him in Germany. What's more, they seem to look to Wilhelm – the son and brother who left them for America – as the key to their salvation when internal family disagreements or conflicts arise. Only Wilhelm's return would ensure that family members would get along and solve related issues, they seem to believe, even though they haven't seen him since he was in his 20s decades ago, and only know of him and his life through an occasional letter.

Probably they look up to Wilhelm for precisely that reason – that he not only had the desire to seek a better life but that he took steps to make it happen, and therefore is living in the New World that seemed to beckon to so many Germans of the day. Friends and acquaintances also look up to him as an example of what is possible for them as they inquire about joining him in America. Family and friends alike see him as someone who has successfully moved beyond life in Sayda and its relative lack of new opportunity.

On the other hand, it is hard to believe that his closest family members in Sayda do not harbor at least some ill will for him, perhaps dismissing him to some degree for selfishly shirking his familial duty, leaving his widowed father and not-yet-teenage younger sister and brother to somehow manage the family farm while he and a young adult sister sought a new life elsewhere. Surprisingly, there is no evidence of this in their letters to him. Instead, their reverence for him seems to grow stronger through the years, and continues even later through younger family members not yet born when he left Sayda.

The letters also illustrate that Wilhelm, no doubt like many other immigrants, becomes a man of two worlds, with separate families with different needs on the two of them. Neither family knows much of the other. Wilhelm's father and siblings in Germany never meet his wife and children, who entered his life after he came to Texas. Likewise, his children and wife know little of his father and his siblings in Germany. He could be torn by the demands of the two groups, but refuses to allow that, despite pleas from his father and German siblings to become more involved in their lives. He is obviously more committed to his family in Texas, a bond that seems stronger than ever in later years after he visits his German homeland, where he finds a disagreeably fine lifestyle that makes him long for his more simple life in Texas.

Left unexplained is why – why Wilhelm and his sister left what must have been a fairly comfortable life in Sayda for Texas. Certainly historians have offered wide and general views about why people like them left the German states in the 19th century. For some, it was political dissent. For others, it was the hype and spin of promoters. And a spate of poor crops or a poor economy had its effect on still more. We have no indication which – if any – of these spurred Wilhelm and his sister. But we know that they decided to travel thousands of miles for months in a small ship for an unsettled country where living was hard, and that they had no thought of ever returning to their homeland. Few among us today would have such courage and commitment.

Appendix A
Relevant Family of Wilhelm F. Kempe

1 Karl Gottlieb Kempe (1774 – 1851)
..   +Christiane Dorothea Eilenberger (1777 – 1847)
.... 2 August Friedrich Kempe (1802 – 1884)
....   +Christiane Frederike Hoepfner (1806 – 1846)
.................3 ***WILHELM FRIEDRICH KEMPE*** (1828 – 1920)
....   +Frederike Laas (1840 – 1895)
....   4 Auguste Emma "Emma" Kempe (1861 – 1942)
....   +Paul Grasshoff (1859 – 1927)
....   4 Wilhelm Friedrich Kempe Jr. (1862 – 1949)
....   +Helena Rabe
....   4 Herman Heinrich Kempe (1864 – 1935)
....   +Sophia Lockman
....   4 Amalie Dorothea Kempe (1867 – 1938)
....   +Henry Thulemeyer
....   4 Carl Edward Kempe (1868 – 1872)
....   4 Emilia Kempe (1868 – 1872)
....   4 Henriette Bertha Kempe (1870 – 1882)
....   4 August Bernhard "Ben" Kempe (1874 – 1957)
....   +Maggie McGill
....   4 Paul Alvin Kempe (1876 – 1938)
....   +Anna Kasper
.................3 Auguste Clementine "Gustel" Kempe (1834 – 1870)
....   +John [Johann] Mayer (1831 – 1876)
....   4 Emma Mayer (1858 – 1919)
....   +Charles Brackenbusch
....   *2nd Husband of Emma Mayer:
....   +Henry Brackenbusch
....   4 Bertha Mayer (1861 – 1946)
....   +Gustav Backhaus
....   4 Mary Margaret Mayer (1864 – 1944)
....   +Henry Bernhard Schmiedekamp
....   4 Anna Mayer (1868 – 1935)
....   +Michael Carl Feist
.................3 Anna Bertha "Bertha" Kempe (1844 – 1903)
....   +August Dietel
....   4 Maria Dietel
....   +Marcus Rudolph
....   4 Karl Dietel (? – 1903)
.................3 Alwin Clemens Kempe (1846 – 1876)
.... 2 Amalie Ernestine Kempe (1813 – 1872)
....   +Johann Heinrich Ernst Weigel
.................3 Edward Weigel
.................3 Hermann Weigel
.................3 Christel Weigel
....   +Peterlein
.................3 Maria Weigel
.................3 Clementine Weigel
....   +Friedrich Einert
.................3 Mienel Weigel

Appendix B
Census Records

These summaries provide only key information from each respective census. The original census records often offer additional details.

Wilhelm's age is wrong in both the 1860 and the 1870 censuses. Born in 1828, he was 32 in 1860 and 42 in 1870. Even so, other data allows verification that the households listed here are those of Wilhelm F. Kempe, the 1854 immigrant from Sayda in what then was the Kingdom of Saxony.

1860 – Austin County, Texas
(July 23, 1860)
Cat Springs, New Ulm, and Industry
Industry Post Office

Name	Age	Occupation	Real Estate	Personal Estate	Birthplace	Married within past year
W. Kemprg	29	Farmer		$300	Germany	yes
F. (wife)	18				Germany	yes

1870 – Fayette County, Texas
(October 11, 1870)
Between Hallettsville Road and Buckner's Creek
Pin Oak Post Office

Name	Age	Occupation	Real Estate	Personal Estate	Birthplace
Kempe, Wm.	50	Farmer	$1,500	$600	Saxony
Frederika	30	Keeps House			Saxony
Emma	9				Texas
Wm.	7				Texas
Herman	6				Texas
Emilia (twin)	3				Texas
Carl (twin)	3				Texas
Bertha	1/12				Texas

Notes:
The 1870 census also indicated that Wilhelm and Frederike could not read and could not write. Letters to and from them in German indicate otherwise. Possibly the census information indicates that they could not read or write in English.

1880 – Fayette County, Texas
(July 5, 1880)
Enumeration District 164; Justice Precincts 5, 6, and 1

Name	Age	Occupation	Birthplace	Birthplace of Father	Birthplace of Mother
Campe, William	48	Farmer	[illegible]	Saxony	Saxony
Friederika	40	Keeps House	Anhalt	Anhalt	Anhalt
Emma	19		Texas	Saxony	Anhalt
Wilhelm	18	Farmer	Texas	Saxony	Anhalt
Herman	16	Farmer	Texas	Saxony	Anhalt
Amalie	13		Texas	Saxony	Anhalt
Bertha	9		Texas	Saxony	Anhalt
Bernhard	7		Texas	Saxony	Anhalt
Paul	4		Texas	Saxony	Anhalt

Notes:
The surname Kempe was obviously misspelled as "Campe" by the census taker.
Wilhelm ("William") would have been 52 in 1880, not 48.
Value of estate was not requested information for the 1880 census.
Twins Emilia and Karl, born in 1868, both died in 1872 – one in January and the other in December.

1900 – Fayette County, Texas
(June 4, 1900)
Enumeration District 49, Precinct 8

Name	Age	Date of Birth	Occupation	Year of Immigration	Birthplace	Can Read, Write, Speak English
Kempe, William	37	June 1862	Farmer		Texas	Yes
Lina	34	Apr. 1866			Texas	Yes
Alfred	11	Oct. 1888			Texas	Yes
Manda	8	Dec 1891			Texas	
Edwin	7	Apr. 1893			Texas	
Laura	5	Apr. 1895			Texas	
Benjamin	3	Mar. 1897			Texas	
Herbert	11/12	June 1899			Texas	
Wilhelm	71	Oct. 1828		1854	Germany	Yes

1910 – Fayette County, Texas
(April 29, 1910)
Enumeration District 66; Justice Precinct 6

Name	Age	Occupation	Birthplace	Birthplace of Father	Birthplace of Mother	Language Spoken
Ben A.	36	Farmer	Texas	Germany	Germany	English
Maggie	32	None	Texas	Mississippi	Texas	English
Ben	9	None	Texas	Texas	Texas	English
William F.	83	None	Germany	Germany	Germany	English

1920 – Jim Wells County, Texas
(January 9, 1920)
Enumeration District 107; Precinct 1

Name	Age	Occupation	Birthplace	Establishment in which at work	Employer, Wage Worker, or Working on Own Account
Kempe, Ben. A	46	Stockfarmer	Texas	Farm	O.A.
Maggie M.	41	None	Texas		
Bennie W.	18	Student	Texas	University	
Frederick W.	92	None	Germany		

Notes:
Wilhelm, identified here as "Frederick," died on February 22, 1920 – less than two months after the January 9 census date.

Appendix C
Tax Records

Property tax data from the 19th century details Wilhelm Kempe's ability to prosper in Texas after the Civil War. As indicated in this data summary (see table, next page), the value of his estate increased more than three-fold from $846 in 1866 to $2,700 by 1883.

To give appropriate perspective to those amounts, and to know how they might compare to property valuations today, monetary inflation must be taken into account. Fortunately, online inflation calculators abound on the Internet.

Those calculators indicate that the $846 value of Wilhelm's property in 1867 was equivalent to $21,745 in 2008.

Also, the $2,700 value of his estate in 1883 was equivalent to $53,538 in 2008.

Wilhelm F. Kempe
Summary of Fayette County Tax Records

Year	Land Acres-Value	Personal Property Horses & Mules-Value	Cattle-Value	Misc.-Value	Total Value
1866	100-$500	n.a.	n.a.	n.a.	n.a.
1867	150-$650	2-$50	12-$36	$110	$846
1868	155-$575	3-$75	12-$36	$130	$816
1869	155-$575	4-$100	20-$60	$125	$860
1870	n.a.	n.a.	n.a.	n.a.	n.a.
1871	155-$880	n.a.	n.a.	n.a.	n.a.
1872	205-$920	5-$100	24-$130	2 sheep-$2 Other-$2	$1,154
1873	205-$920	5-$125	19-$110	5 sheep-$5 Other-$15	$1,175
1874	205-$835	6-$150	17-$90	$96	$1,171
1875	205-$940	6-$150	20-$80	$95	$1,265
1876	305-$1,400	6-$120	25-$100	$80	$1,700
1877	n.a.	n.a.	n.a.	n.a.	n.a.
1878	305-$1,235	5-$100	15/$60	Carriage-$30 5 hogs-$10 Other-$63	$1,498
1879	305-$1,235	6-$120	20-$84	Carriage-$35 8 hogs-$16 Other-$64	$1,550
1880	305-$1,340	6-$120	25-$125	Carriage-$30 8 hogs-$16 25 sheep-$50 Other-$39	$1,720
1881	305-$1,340	5-$100	20-$100	Carriage-$25 Tools-$50 5 sheep-$10 8 hogs-$16 Other-$27	$1,668
1882	494-$1,989	7-$150	25-$175	Carriage-$25 Tools-$90 10 sheep-$25 4 hogs-$8 Other-$8	$2,465
1883	500-$2,090	7-$175	25-$200	2 carriages-$75 Tools-$50 10 sheep-$15 4 hogs-$10 Other-$5	$2,700

Appendix D
Locations in Germany

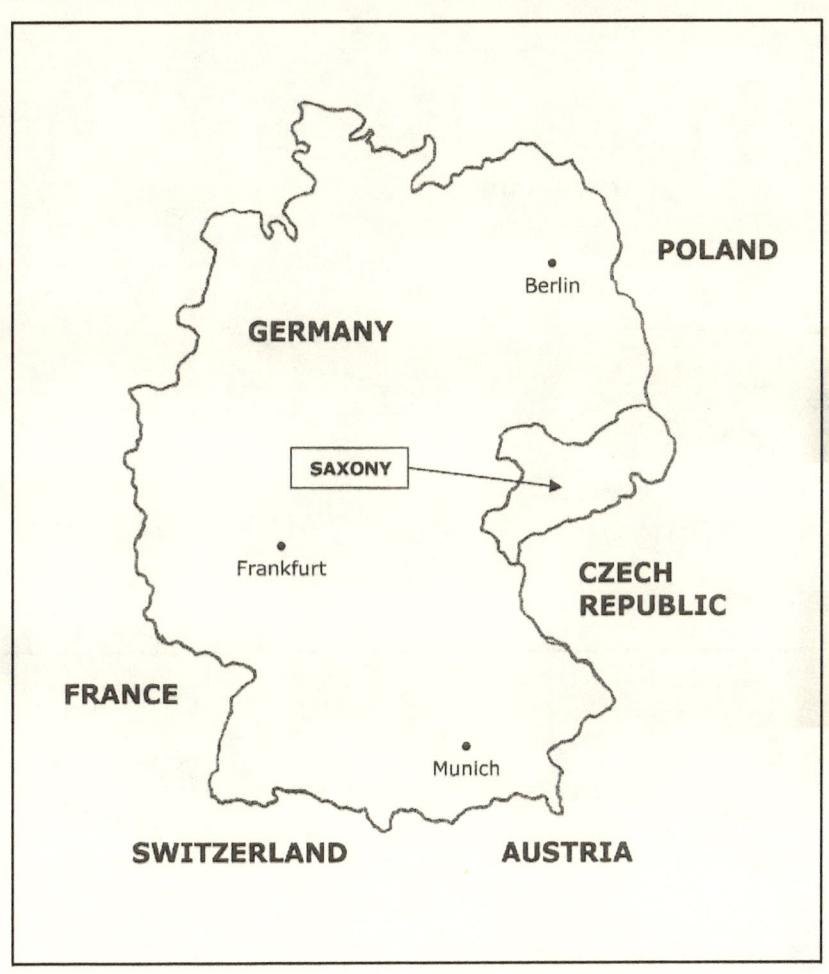

Appendix E
Locations in Texas

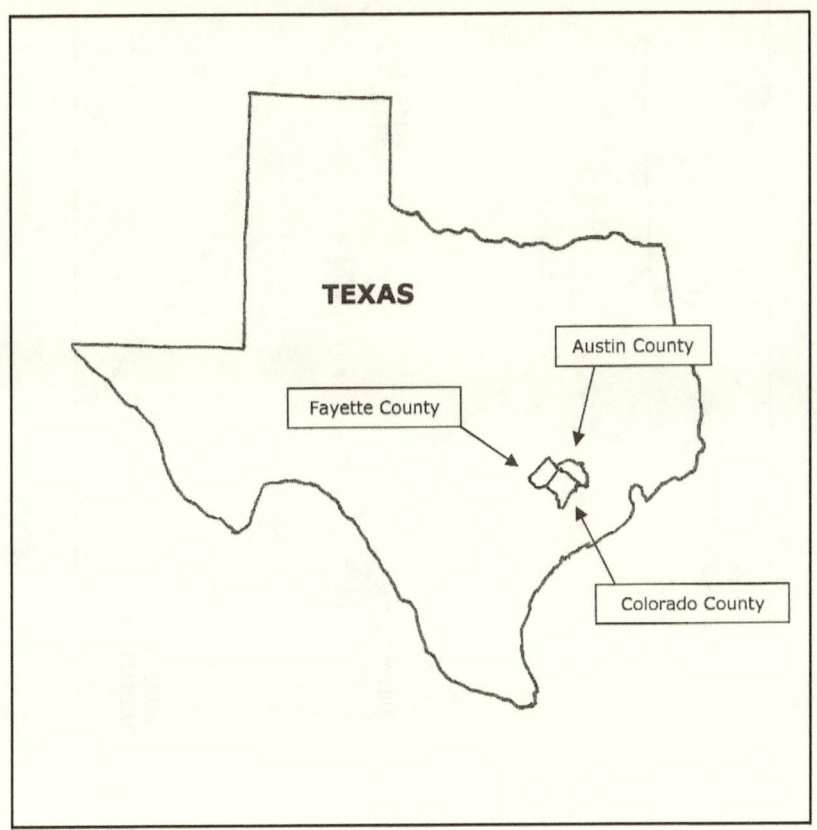

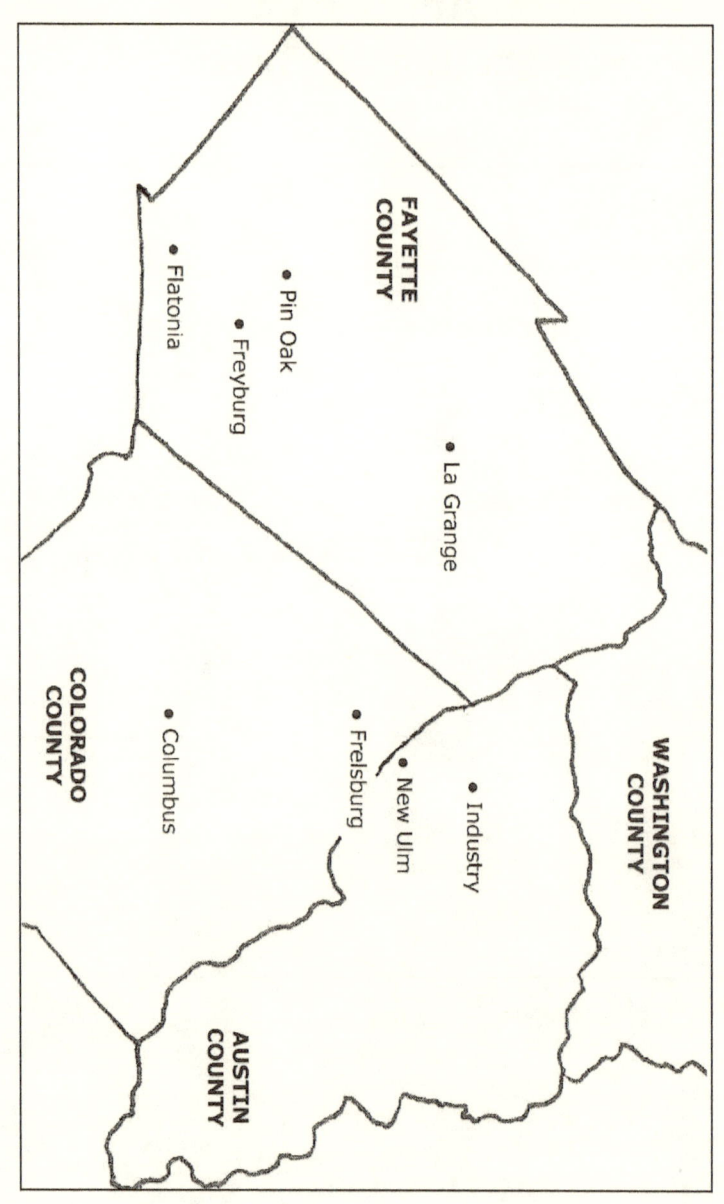

Appendix F
Letter from Hermann Weigel

Only one of the original Kempe letters is known to survive. It's the November 12, 1872 letter to Wilhelm from his cousin, Hermann Weigel.

This letter was not part of the original collection of letters that were translated into English in the early 1960s. Instead, it was in the possession of another, smaller group of Kempe descendants unknown to the group that produced the original collection. This smaller group descended from Wilhelm's eldest daughter, Emma Kempe Grasshoff, and her only daughter, Mary Grasshoff Kuessel.

The good physical condition of this particular letter allows higher quality photocopies, which in turn should allow more accurate translations of the old German script. Within the past 10 years, the author has sought and obtained English translations of the letter from two translators. Although their interpretations agree in general, they sometimes vary in detail, illustrating either the difficulty in translating the old German script or the different skills of the translators.

A careful review of the letter and the translations by this author, who admittedly has no particular knowledge of this type of script, suggests that Hermann Weigel, the letter writer, sometimes appears to write a letter of the alphabet in different ways within the same letter. That practice adds significantly to difficulties in translating the letter, and suggests that differences in translations are the result of those types of confusing factors rather than inadequacies in the skills of the translators.

The letter's four pages follow.

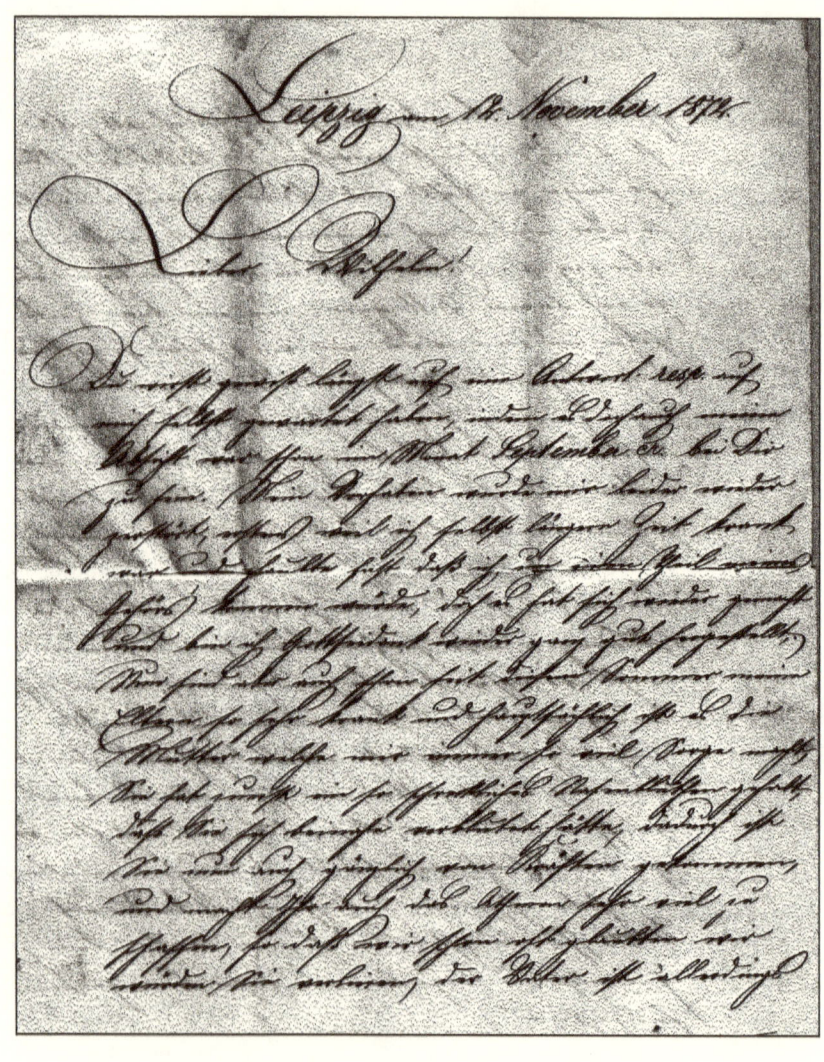

Hermann Weigel to Wilhelm Kempe, November 12, 1872 (page 1 of letter)

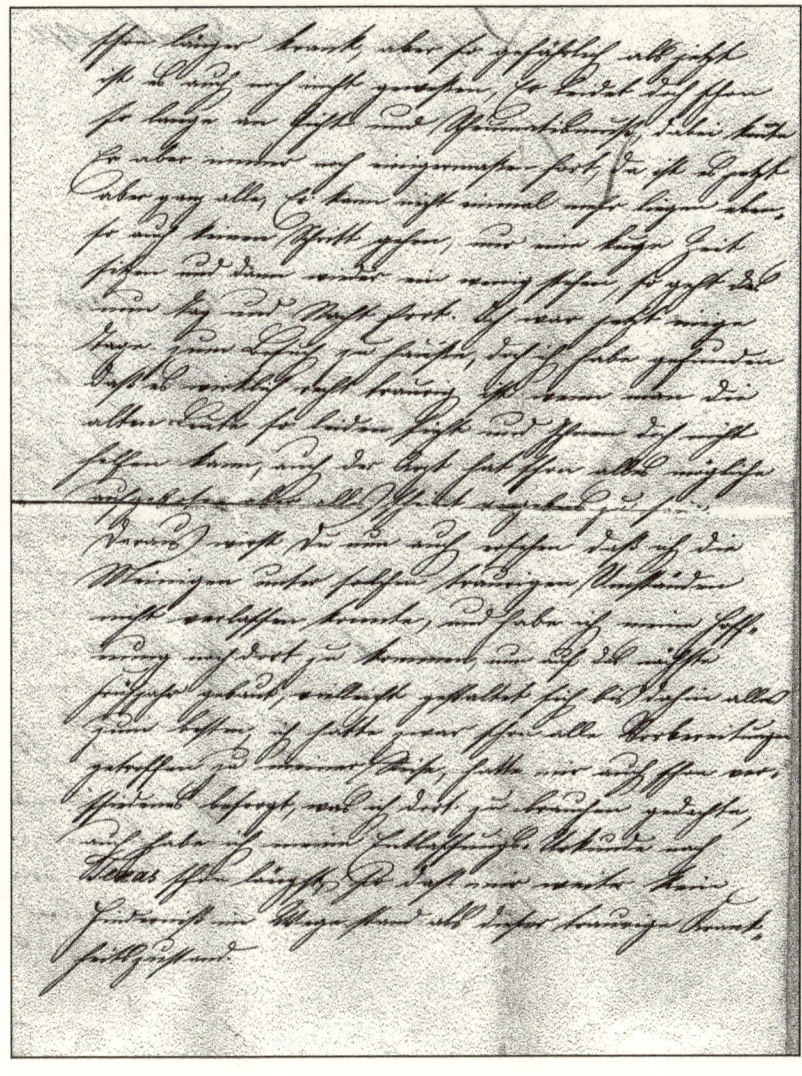

Hermann Weigel to Wilhelm Kempe, November 12, 1872 (page 2 of letter)

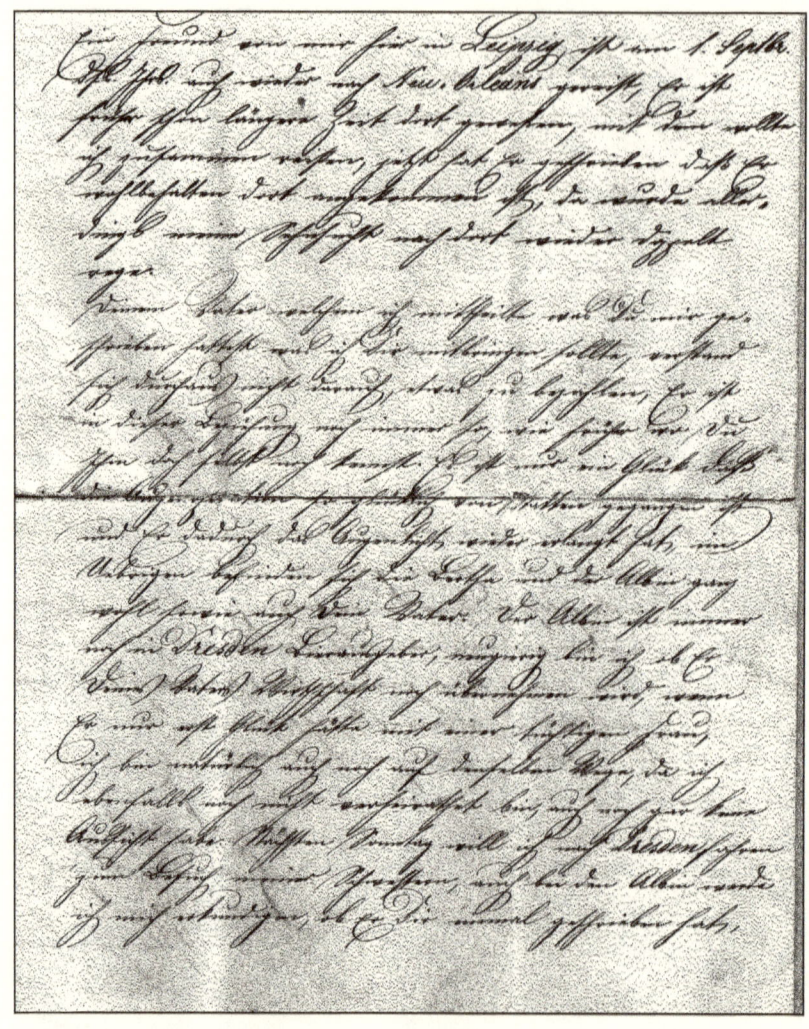

Hermann Weigel to Wilhelm Kempe, November 12, 1872 (page 3 of letter)

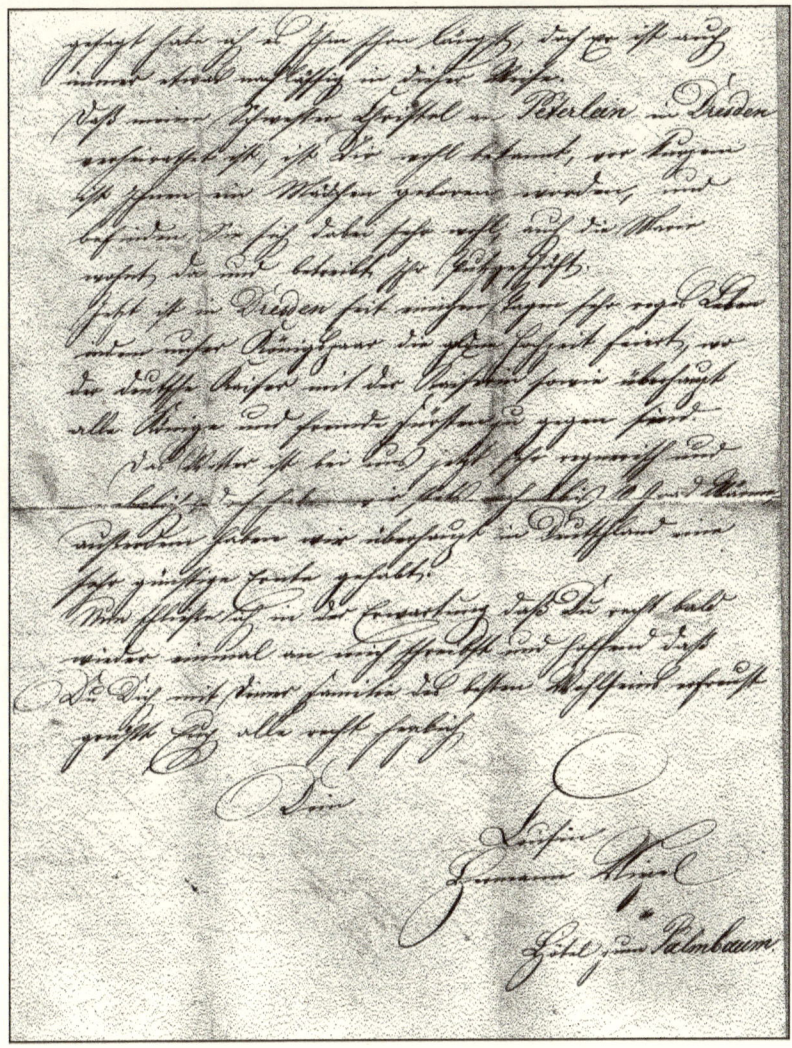

Hermann Weigel to Wilhelm Kempe, November 12, 1872 (page 4 of letter)

Acknowledgements

This book is based in large measure on the English translations obtained in the early 1960s by Mr. and Mrs. Charles W. Kempe, and a subsequent compilation of those translations by Mr. and Mrs. Paul O. Kempe. Without their interest and efforts to preserve these irreplaceable pieces of family history, the historical insights it provides would have been lost. The preface to the original 1960s-era compilation, reproduced nearly verbatim here, notes the contributions of others as well:

> *"An absorbing year of research into the lives of the William Frederick Kempe family and his father's family, August Frederick Kempe of Sayda, Germany, has taken place since the reunion of the "Kempe Klan" June 18, 1961. These historic and revealing letters written between the years 1863 and 1903 had been preserved by Mrs. Amalia Kempe Thulemeyer. On the death of Mrs. Amalia Kempe Thulemeyer, Mrs. Maggie Thulemeyer Stierling, and Mrs. Mayme Thulemeyer Outlaw found these letters stored away in the attic in a trunk, in the family home in Flatonia, Texas. Many letters had deteriorated with time and squirrels had nibbled away at others. Mrs. Maggie Thulemeyer Stierling, in turn, saved these letters and through her interest and generosity, let Paul O. Kempe photostat them for use in this folder. Then with aroused interest, untiring efforts and expense, Mr. and Mrs. Charles W. Kempe then had the letters translated* [and typed], *then sent them to Paul O. Kempe. He then compiled and sorted this material so that you can read and keep these most interesting and informative letters that give you a glimpse into the past with such a vivid reality that you almost expect a letter from 'Great-great-grandfather August Frederick* [sic]*Kempe, Sayda, Germany' tomorrow.*
>
> *It is with a feeling of pride and admiration that one can unfold these pages of the past and see a father and his son both of strong character, home-loving, religious, and*

---

devoted fathers who worried about their families and
loved life until the end.
    Thank each and every one of you for the contribution
and help that has made this work possible."

Gladys T. Kempe
(Mrs. P. O. Kempe)

Notably, this collection includes one letter that was not part of the original collection. The November 12, 1872 letter to Wilhelm from his cousin Hermann Weigel (see "Appendix F") was in the possession of other relatives – Coy and Norma Ramsey. Their willingness to provide a copy of that letter, which is the only letter that remains clearly legible, helped recent translators ensure the accuracy of names and places.

Also, Velmalene Williams has provided vital information about Wilhelm's brother-in-law John [Johannes] Mayer and the children he fathered with Auguste, Wilhelm's sister. Her interest in the Kempe family and willingness to help is greatly appreciated.

Finally, in my efforts to research, develop, and complete this project, no one has been a better friend or colleague than my wife, Rita Grasshoff. Her contributions are always vital and innumerable.

Bibliography

Books

Biesele, Rudolph Leopold. *The History of the German Settlements in Texas, 1831-1861*. Austin, Texas: Eakin Press, ca.1987

Easley, S. C. *Ships Passenger Lists: Port of Galveston Texas, 1846-1871*. Southern Historical Press, published under the auspices of the Galveston County Genealogical Society, ca.1984.

Farber, James. *Texas, CSA*. New York: The Jackson Company, 1947.

Feuchtwanger, Edgar. *Bismarck*. London: Routledge, 2002.

Flach, Vera. *A Yankee in German-America; Texas Hill Country*. San Antonio, Texas: Naylor Company, 1973

Gish, Theodore and Spuler, Richard, eds. *Eagle in the New World: German immigration to Texas and America*. College Station, Texas: Published for the Texas Committee for the Humanities by Texas A&M University Press, ca. 1986.

Geue, Chester W., and Geue, Ethel H. *A New Land Beckoned: German Immigration to Texas, 1844-1847*. Baltimore, Maryland: Genealogical Publishing Company, 1982, c1966.

Jordan, Terry G. *German Seed in Texas Soil: Immigrant Farmers in Nineteenth-Century Texas*. Austin, Texas: University of Texas Press, 1966, 1975.

Kamphoefner, Walter D. and Helbich, Wolfgang Johannes, eds. *Germans in the Civil War: The Letters They Wrote Home*. Translated by Susan Carter Vogel. UNC Press, 2006.

Lich, Glenn E. *The German Texans*. San Antonio, Texas: The University of Texas at San Antonio Institute of Texan Cultures, 1981; revised, 1996.

McPherson, James. *Battle Cry of Freedom*. Oxford Press: New York, 1988.

Nagel, Charles. *A Boy's Civil War Story*. Philadelphia, Pennsylvania; Dorance and Company, 1935

Schlecht, Friedrich. *On to Texas! A Journey to Texas in 1848*. Translated by Charles Patrick. Manor, Texas: Indio Bravo Press, 1988.

Schünemann, C. *The Emigrant to Texas: A Handbook & Guide*. Bremen, Germany, 1846. Translated by Otto W. Tetzlaff. Burnet, Texas: Eakin Publications, ca.1979

Scott, Robert Nicholson. *The War of the Rebellion: A Compilation of the Official Records of the Union and Confederate Armies*. U.S. War Department, published in Historical Times, 1886.

Tiling, Moritz. *History of the German Element in Texas from 1820-1850*. Houston: Moritz Tiling, 1913

Weyand, Leonie Rummel, and Wade, Houston. *An Early History of Fayette County*. La Grange, Texas: La Grange Journal, 1936

Williamson, D. G. *Bismarck and Germany, 1862-1890*. Longman, 1998.

Articles

Brister, Louis B. "Adelsverein." *The Handbook of Texas Online*. <http://www.tshaonline.org/handbook/online/articles/AA/ufa1.html>

Jordan, Terry G. "Germans." *The Handbook of Texas Online*. <http://www.tshaonline.org/handbook/online/articles/GG/png2.html>

Kamphoefner, Walter D. "New Perspectives on Texas Germans and the Confederacy." *Southwestern Historical Quarterly*, vol. CII, no. 4. April 1999.

Kempe, Mrs. P. O. "Kempe, William Frederick, Sr." *Shiner, Texas: The First 100 Years, 1887-1987*. Dallas: Curtis Media Corp. for Shiner History Book Committee, 1986

Ramos, Mary G. "The Deadly Visitor; Yellow Fever." *Texas Almanac*. February 28, 2009. <http://www.texasalmanac.com/history/highlights/fever/>

Stein, Bill. "Consider the Lily: The Ungilded History of Colorado County, Texas." *Nesbitt Memorial Library Journal*. Columbus, Texas. <http://www.columbustexas.net/library/history/indexlily.htm>

Unpublished Documents

Gladys T. Kempe, ed. *Letters to and from William Frederick Kempe*. Translated by Ms. Dixon of San Antonio, Texas, ca. 1961 (unpublished document exists only as photocopy in possession of an unknown number of Kempe family members and possibly others)

Archival Records

1860 U.S. census, population schedule, Austin County, Texas (various districts, precincts, and families)

1860 U.S. census, population schedule, Colorado County, Texas (various districts, precincts, and families)

1860 U.S. census, population schedule, Fayette County, Texas (various districts, precincts, and families)

1870 U.S. census, population schedule, Austin County, Texas (various districts, precincts, and families)

1870 U.S. census, population schedule, Colorado County, Texas (various districts, precincts, and families)

1870 U.S. census, population schedule, Fayette County, Texas (various districts, precincts, and families)

1880 U.S. census, population schedule, Fayette County, Texas, Enumeration District 164, Precinct Nos. 5, 6, and 1, William Campe [Kempe] household; digital image, Ancestry.com (www.ancestry.com).

1900 U.S. census, population schedule, Fayette County, Texas, Enumeration District 49, Precinct 8, William Kempe household; digital image, Ancestry.com (www.ancestry.com).

1910 U.S. census, population schedule, Fayette County, Texas, Enumeration District 66, Precinct 6, Ben A. Kempe household; digital image, Ancestry.com (www.ancestry.com)

1920 U.S. census, population schedule, Jim Wells County, Texas, Enumeration District 107, Precinct 1, Ben A. Kempe household; digital image, Ancestry.com (www.ancestry.com).

Ancestry.com. *New York Passenger Lists, 1820-1957* [database on-line]. Provo, UT, USA: The Generations Network, Inc., 2006. Original data: Passenger Lists of Vessels Arriving at New York, New York, 1820-1897; (National Archives Microfilm Publication M237, 675 rolls); Records of the U.S. Customs Service, Record Group 36; National Archives, Washington, D.C.

Fayette County property tax records, Fayette County, Texas, 1866-1883, taxpayer Wilhelm F. Kempe; microfilm image, Fayette Heritage Museum and Archives, La Grange, Fayette County, Texas.

Philadelphia Lutheran Church (Der Evangelisch Lutheran Philadelphia Gemeinde), East Navidad community, Fayette County, Texas. Baptismal records, "from 1867 until." Available in copy at Texas Wendish Heritage Society library, Serbin, Lee County, Texas.

Salem Lutheran Church, Freyburg, Fayette County, Texas. Baptismal records, 1869-1904. Available in copy at Texas Wendish Heritage Society library, Serbin, Lee County, Texas.

Trinity Lutheran Church, Frelsburg, Colorado County, Texas. Baptismal records, 1889-1964. Available via Internet from Nesbitt Memorial Library, Columbus, Texas: http://www.columbustexas.net/library/church%20records/trinity%20baptisms%201.htm)

About the Author

Ray Grasshoff is a writer living in Austin, Texas.

Among other interests, he enjoys studying history primarily for the perspective it continues to give current events.

Formerly, he was a public information officer at four State of Texas agencies – the Railroad Commission of Texas, the Texas Water Development Board, the Texas Department of Health's Bureau of Radiation Control, and the Texas Higher Education Coordinating Board.

He has written numerous magazine articles as well, and also edited a weekly newspaper in Schulenburg, Texas, where he grew up.

He holds a journalism degree from Texas A&M University.